OAuth 2.0

James Relington

DEDICATION

This book is dedicated to all the professionals working tirelessly to secure digital identities and protect organizations from ever-evolving threats. To the cybersecurity teams, IT administrators, and identity management experts who ensure safe and seamless access for users—your work is invaluable. And to my family and friends, whose support and encouragement made this journey possible, thank you.

AKNOWLEDGEMENTS

I would like to express my deepest gratitude to everyone who contributed to the creation of this book. To my colleagues and mentors in the cybersecurity and identity management field, your insights and expertise have been invaluable. To the organizations and professionals who shared their experiences and best practices, your contributions have enriched this work. A special thanks to my family and friends for their unwavering support and encouragement throughout this journey. Finally, to the readers, thank you for your interest in identity lifecycle management—may this book help you navigate the evolving landscape of digital security with confidence.

The Fundamentals of OAuth 2.0

OAuth 2.0 is a widely adopted open standard that enables secure, delegated access to resources without requiring users to share their credentials. Rather than a single, rigid protocol, OAuth 2.0 is best understood as a framework that provides developers with a range of options for implementing authorization flows. Its flexibility, scalability, and compatibility with modern application architectures have made it a go-to solution for securing APIs, mobile apps, and web applications. By understanding the core concepts, components, and flows of OAuth 2.0, organizations can implement secure, efficient authorization strategies that meet their specific needs.

At its core, OAuth 2.0 addresses the challenge of granting third-party applications limited access to a user's resources without exposing the user's password or other sensitive credentials. In a traditional model, users might share their username and password directly with a third-party service, relying on that service to handle authentication and authorization securely. This approach not only introduces significant security risks—such as credential reuse, storage, and possible theft—but also creates a poor user experience. OAuth 2.0 eliminates the need for direct credential sharing by introducing a token-based system. This system allows resource owners to delegate specific permissions to third-party clients while keeping their primary credentials private and under the control of a trusted authorization server.

OAuth 2.0 defines several roles that participate in its flows. The resource owner is the user or entity that holds the data or resources being accessed. The client is the application or service that seeks access to those resources on behalf of the resource owner. The resource server is the system hosting the protected resources, and the authorization server is the entity that authenticates the resource owner and issues tokens to the client. By separating these roles, OAuth 2.0 ensures that the client never directly handles the resource owner's credentials. Instead, the client interacts with the authorization server, which acts as a trusted intermediary that can verify the resource owner's identity and grant appropriate access tokens.

A central concept in OAuth 2.0 is the use of access tokens. An access token is a time-limited credential issued by the authorization server that the client can present to the resource server. This token specifies the scope of access, such as what data the client can retrieve or what actions it can perform. The resource server validates the token and determines whether to allow the requested operation. By issuing tokens with defined scopes and expiration times, OAuth 2.0 provides fine-grained control over access permissions and reduces the impact of compromised tokens.

In addition to access tokens, OAuth 2.0 can leverage refresh tokens. Refresh tokens are long-lived credentials that allow the client to obtain new access tokens without requiring the resource owner to reauthenticate. This mechanism enhances user experience by enabling persistent access without repeatedly prompting the user, while still ensuring that access tokens remain short-lived. If a refresh token is ever compromised, it can be revoked by the authorization server, effectively cutting off access without affecting the resource owner's main credentials.

OAuth 2.0 provides multiple grant types, each designed for different scenarios. The authorization code grant is commonly used by server-based applications and involves a two-step process where the client first receives an authorization code from the authorization server and then exchanges it for an access token. This grant type is considered secure because the authorization code is transmitted via a user-agent (such as a browser), while the actual token exchange occurs on a backend server. The implicit grant, on the other hand, is designed for single-page applications (SPAs) and mobile apps where the client cannot securely store secrets. In this flow, access tokens are issued directly without an intermediate code exchange, making it simpler but potentially less secure in certain contexts. The client credentials grant allows machine-to-machine communication, where the client authenticates directly with the authorization server using its own credentials. Finally, the resource owner password credentials grant is used in cases where the resource owner's username and password are provided directly to the client, though this is generally discouraged unless no better alternative exists.

OAuth 2.0's modular design allows it to adapt to a wide range of use cases and deployment scenarios. Its token-based approach not only enhances security by avoiding credential sharing but also aligns well with modern application architectures that rely on APIs, microservices, and distributed systems. By supporting various grant types and flows, OAuth 2.0 gives developers the flexibility to implement the framework in ways that best suit their technical requirements and user experiences. This versatility has made OAuth 2.0 a cornerstone of secure, scalable authorization in today's interconnected digital landscape.

Understanding Authorization Flows

Authorization flows are at the heart of OAuth 2.0's flexibility, enabling developers to securely delegate access across a wide range of applications and devices. These flows determine how an application, known as a client, obtains tokens that grant it access to a user's resources. By carefully selecting and implementing the appropriate authorization flow, organizations can ensure secure, efficient interactions between resource owners, authorization servers, and resource servers, all while maintaining a seamless user experience. Understanding these flows is essential for making informed architectural decisions and achieving secure integration.

The authorization code flow is one of the most commonly used OAuth 2.0 authorization flows. It's well-suited for applications that can securely store secrets, such as web applications with server-side components. In this flow, the client directs the user to the authorization server's authorization endpoint, where the user authenticates and grants consent. Once the user approves the request, the authorization server issues an authorization code and redirects it back to the client's server. The client then exchanges this code for an access token by securely communicating with the authorization server's token endpoint. Because the access token is obtained through a back-channel communication rather than directly in the browser, this flow helps prevent token leakage and provides a strong foundation for secure access to protected resources.

The implicit flow, on the other hand, was originally designed for browser-based clients that couldn't securely store secrets, such as single-page applications (SPAs). In this flow, the client receives an access token directly from the authorization endpoint after the user grants consent. This eliminates the need for a server-to-server token exchange, but it also introduces some security considerations. Since the access token is returned in the browser, it is more exposed to potential interception. For this reason, the implicit flow is now considered less secure than other flows and is often replaced with more robust alternatives, such as using the authorization code flow with PKCE (Proof Key for Code Exchange) in modern SPAs.

Another important flow is the client credentials flow. This flow is used for machine-to-machine interactions where no user is involved. Instead of redirecting a user for approval, the client itself authenticates directly with the authorization server using its own credentials—such as a client ID and client secret—to obtain an access token. This is particularly useful for backend services, APIs, and automation tasks that need to communicate securely without a user's involvement. Because it does not rely on user authentication, the client credentials flow simplifies many interactions while still ensuring that access is properly scoped and controlled through tokens.

The resource owner password credentials flow, while available, is generally discouraged in favor of other approaches. In this flow, the client collects the resource owner's username and password directly and submits them to the authorization server in exchange for an access token. While this might seem straightforward, it comes with significant security risks, as it requires the client to handle sensitive user credentials. This flow is typically used only when no other flow can meet the application's needs, and even then, it should be implemented with caution and strong security controls in place.

Recent advancements in OAuth 2.0 have introduced enhancements like PKCE, which was originally designed for public clients such as mobile apps. PKCE adds an additional layer of security to the authorization code flow by requiring the client to generate a unique code challenge and code verifier pair. During the initial request, the client sends the code challenge to the authorization server. When it later exchanges the authorization code for an access token, it must provide the corresponding code verifier. This ensures that even if the authorization code is intercepted, it cannot be exchanged without the correct code verifier, effectively mitigating certain attack vectors. PKCE has become a best practice for modern applications, including SPAs and mobile apps, where traditional client secrets cannot be securely stored.

When selecting an authorization flow, organizations must consider factors such as the type of application, the level of security required, and the user experience they want to provide. Web applications that can maintain secure server-side storage are often best served by the authorization code flow, which offers a high degree of security and flexibility. For server-to-server communication, the client credentials flow provides a straightforward, secure mechanism. For mobile or SPA environments, using the authorization code flow with PKCE combines strong security with a simplified user experience. Understanding these flows and their appropriate use cases allows developers to design authentication and authorization systems that align with both security standards and user expectations.

Each authorization flow in OAuth 2.0 is tailored to address specific scenarios, offering a variety of options for securely managing access. By thoroughly understanding these flows, developers can choose the best approach for their applications, ensuring that both security and user experience are maintained across different environments and use cases.

The Role of Access Tokens

Access tokens play a central role in the OAuth 2.0 authorization framework, serving as the key mechanism by which clients gain secure access to protected resources. At their core, access tokens are time-limited, credential-like objects issued by an authorization server. They allow a client—such as a web application, mobile app, or API client—to authenticate its requests to a resource server without directly handling user credentials. By leveraging access tokens, OAuth 2.0 achieves both security and convenience, providing a scalable way to control and delegate access across diverse environments.

Access tokens are designed to encapsulate specific permissions, often referred to as scopes, that dictate what resources the client can access and what actions it can perform. For example, a token might permit reading user profile information but not modifying it, or allow accessing a user's calendar but not their email. By embedding these permissions directly into the token, resource servers can make fine-grained access control decisions without needing to consult additional databases or perform complex lookups. This self-contained nature of access tokens simplifies the overall architecture, making them a versatile and efficient means of enforcing authorization policies.

One of the key advantages of access tokens is their short lifespan. Unlike long-lived credentials or passwords, access tokens are typically valid only for a limited period—often just minutes or hours. This limited validity period significantly reduces the impact of a compromised token. If an attacker manages to intercept an access token, the window of opportunity is brief. Additionally, access tokens can be revoked by the authorization server if suspicious activity is detected. This ephemeral nature of access tokens ensures that they remain a lower-risk mechanism for granting temporary access, aligning with security best practices.

Access tokens also provide flexibility in how they are structured and transmitted. Many modern OAuth implementations use JSON Web Tokens (JWTs) as the format for access tokens. A JWT is a compact, URL-safe token that can include claims about the user, the client, the scopes granted, and the token's expiration time. Since JWTs are digitally signed, resource servers can validate the token's integrity without needing to contact the authorization server each time. This self-verifying property enables faster and more efficient processing of requests, particularly in high-traffic environments. However, it's important to note that not all access tokens are JWTs; some implementations use opaque tokens that require the resource server to perform a lookup at the authorization server. The choice of token format depends on the specific requirements of the environment and the trade-offs between scalability and validation complexity.

Another important characteristic of access tokens is that they are bearer tokens. This means that possession of the token is enough to gain access to the specified resources, similar to cash or a movie ticket. While this design makes token usage simple and straightforward, it also highlights the importance of securing tokens during transmission and storage. Tokens should always be transmitted over secure channels (e.g., HTTPS) to prevent interception. Additionally, clients must store tokens securely, using techniques such as secure storage APIs on mobile devices or environment variables on server-side applications. By treating tokens as sensitive credentials, organizations can minimize the risk of unauthorized access.

In many scenarios, access tokens are paired with refresh tokens to extend their usability. While access tokens are short-lived, refresh tokens are long-lived and can be used to obtain new access tokens without requiring the user to reauthenticate. This approach enhances the user experience by reducing login prompts while still maintaining the security benefits of short-lived access tokens. Refresh tokens are typically stored more securely than access tokens and may be subject to stricter revocation policies. By using both access and refresh tokens, organizations can strike a balance between security and user convenience, ensuring that clients maintain ongoing access without exposing long-term credentials.

Resource servers rely on access tokens to simplify and standardize authorization checks. When a client presents an access token, the resource server validates it—often by verifying its signature or consulting a token introspection endpoint. Once validated, the resource server uses the information within the token (such as scopes or claims) to determine whether the requested action is permitted. This consistent process allows resource servers to enforce policies without needing to store or manage user credentials themselves. By decoupling authentication and authorization, access tokens make it easier to build scalable, distributed systems where different components can operate independently while maintaining a secure and cohesive access control model.

The use of access tokens is not limited to a single application or service. In many cases, tokens are used across multiple resource servers or even different organizations in a federated environment. For example, an enterprise might issue tokens that grant access to both internal APIs and third-party SaaS platforms. By standardizing on access tokens, organizations can create unified authentication and authorization experiences that simplify integration, reduce duplication of effort, and improve security posture. This versatility makes access tokens a foundational element of modern identity and access management frameworks.

Understanding the role of access tokens in OAuth 2.0 is critical for building secure and scalable authorization systems. By leveraging their time-limited nature, structured format, and flexible validation methods, developers can create efficient workflows that balance security, usability, and performance. Access tokens enable seamless delegation of access, helping organizations manage complex ecosystems of clients, users, and protected resources in a secure and efficient manner.

Refresh Tokens and Their Purpose

Refresh tokens are a fundamental component of OAuth 2.0, designed to provide clients with a seamless, secure way to maintain long-term access to protected resources. Unlike access tokens, which are short-lived and must be regularly renewed, refresh tokens allow a client to request new access tokens from the authorization server without re-prompting the resource owner for authentication. By using refresh tokens, organizations can enhance user convenience, maintain secure session continuity, and reduce the risk associated with long-lived credentials.

The primary purpose of a refresh token is to support session persistence. In a typical OAuth 2.0 flow, a user authenticates with an identity provider, and the authorization server issues an access token that grants the client temporary permission to access a protected resource. Since access tokens are intentionally short-lived—often expiring in minutes or hours—they ensure that any stolen or compromised tokens have a limited lifespan. This improves security but creates a challenge for maintaining a smooth user experience. Without refresh tokens, the user would need to re-authenticate frequently, which can be inconvenient, especially for applications that need continuous access to resources, such as background services or long-running processes. Refresh tokens solve this problem by allowing the client to quietly obtain new access tokens from the authorization server, ensuring uninterrupted access without user intervention.

Another key role of refresh tokens is reducing the frequency of user authentication requests. When a refresh token is issued, it typically has a longer lifespan than an access token. This means the client can request new access tokens as long as the refresh token remains valid, avoiding repeated prompts for the user's credentials. For example, a mobile application that uses OAuth 2.0 can store a refresh token securely and periodically exchange it for new access tokens in the background. The user only sees the initial login prompt, and afterward, the application silently refreshes tokens as needed, providing a seamless, uninterrupted experience.

Refresh tokens also contribute to security by minimizing the exposure of sensitive credentials. In many cases, the user's primary credentials (such as username and password) are only provided during the initial authentication process. Once authenticated, the user's credentials are no longer involved in subsequent token exchanges. Instead, the refresh token takes on the role of granting ongoing access. If the refresh token is compromised, its scope and validity can be tightly controlled, and the authorization server can quickly revoke it. This means that even in the event of token theft, the damage is limited compared to what might occur if long-lived access tokens or stored passwords were compromised.

The use of refresh tokens also aligns well with modern application architectures and distributed systems. In environments where multiple microservices or APIs interact, having short-lived access tokens combined with long-lived refresh tokens simplifies token management and enhances scalability. Instead of each service managing long-term credentials or persistent user sessions, they can rely on a centralized authorization server to issue new access tokens as needed. This reduces the complexity of individual services, centralizes security policies, and ensures that expired tokens are quickly replaced without interrupting the user's session.

From a compliance perspective, refresh tokens help organizations meet stringent security and regulatory requirements. Many compliance frameworks, such as GDPR or HIPAA, emphasize the importance of minimizing the lifespan of sensitive credentials and ensuring that access is tightly controlled. By using short-lived access tokens and refreshing them as needed, organizations demonstrate that they are taking active steps to secure sensitive data and maintain a robust authentication process. Refresh tokens also allow for real-time revocation, giving administrators the ability to immediately cut off access if suspicious activity is detected or if a user's account needs to be disabled.

To maintain the security of refresh tokens, it's critical to store them securely and follow best practices. Clients should use secure storage mechanisms that prevent unauthorized access to tokens. On mobile devices, for instance, applications can leverage secure storage APIs or hardware-based key storage solutions. On servers, refresh tokens should be kept in secure, encrypted environments, with access tightly restricted. Additionally, when a refresh token is no longer needed—for example, if a user logs out or their session is terminated—it should be revoked and removed from storage. Implementing these safeguards ensures that refresh tokens remain a secure method for maintaining long-term access.

Refresh tokens can also support advanced use cases and flexible authentication workflows. For instance, an application may issue refresh tokens with varying lifespans based on the user's role, the client's level of trust, or the sensitivity of the requested resource. This granularity allows organizations to enforce stricter policies for certain types of access while maintaining a user-friendly experience for less sensitive operations. Furthermore, refresh tokens can be combined with multi-factor authentication or adaptive authentication measures, providing an additional layer of security before granting new access tokens. By tailoring refresh token policies to the specific needs of the environment, organizations can strike the right balance between security and convenience.

In sum, refresh tokens play a crucial role in maintaining secure, uninterrupted access to protected resources in an OAuth 2.0 environment. By reducing the need for frequent user authentication, limiting credential exposure, and supporting scalable architectures, refresh tokens enhance both security and user experience. As a best practice, organizations should implement secure storage, enforce appropriate token lifespans, and regularly audit their refresh token policies to ensure that this essential component of the OAuth framework continues to deliver both security and convenience.

Exploring Token Lifecycles

Token lifecycles are a crucial aspect of any OAuth 2.0 implementation, directly impacting the balance between security and user convenience. By carefully managing the lifespan of tokens, organizations can minimize the risk of misuse while ensuring a seamless user experience. Understanding how tokens are issued, how long they remain valid, and what happens when they expire is essential for designing a secure, efficient authorization architecture that meets both business and security requirements.

At the core of the OAuth 2.0 framework are two primary types of tokens: access tokens and refresh tokens. Access tokens are short-lived credentials used to authenticate requests to a resource server. They are typically valid for only a brief period—ranging from a few minutes to several hours—ensuring that if an attacker intercepts an access token, their window of opportunity is limited. The short lifespan of access tokens forces clients to obtain new tokens regularly, making it harder for compromised tokens to be exploited over the long term. This strategy enhances security by reducing the impact of token theft and encouraging the use of current, validated credentials.

Refresh tokens, on the other hand, have a longer lifecycle. Their primary role is to allow the client to obtain new access tokens without requiring the user to reauthenticate. This is especially useful in applications that need ongoing access to resources over extended periods, such as mobile apps or long-running background services. By using refresh tokens, these applications can maintain a smooth user experience without repeatedly prompting the user for their credentials. However, since refresh tokens are long-lived, they must be carefully managed. If a refresh token is compromised, it could be used to issue multiple access tokens, potentially extending the attacker's ability to access resources. To mitigate this risk, organizations can implement token rotation, frequent auditing, and secure storage practices to ensure that refresh tokens are not easily accessible or misused.

The lifecycle of an access token begins when the client requests authorization from the resource owner. Once the resource owner approves the request, the authorization server issues an access token along with, optionally, a refresh token. The access token is then used to authenticate subsequent requests to the resource server. As the token nears its expiration time, the client may use the associated refresh token to request a new access token. This process repeats as long as the refresh token remains valid, extending the lifecycle of the authorization session without requiring the user to log in again. When the refresh token eventually expires, or if it is revoked, the client must prompt the user to reauthenticate, starting the cycle anew.

Token expiration is a critical component of the token lifecycle. By setting a short expiration time for access tokens, organizations ensure that even if a token is stolen, its usability is severely limited. Once an access token expires, any attempt to use it will result in an error from the resource server, prompting the client to request a fresh token. This approach helps maintain strong security while still allowing clients to perform their tasks without constant user intervention. If a client is compromised, short-lived tokens also reduce the amount of time that an attacker can use them before they become invalid.

Refresh tokens, while long-lived, are not intended to last indefinitely. Many OAuth 2.0 implementations enforce policies that cause refresh tokens to expire after a certain period, typically ranging from days to weeks. This limits the risk associated with a compromised refresh token, as it eventually becomes invalid even if the user has not logged out or reauthenticated. Organizations may also choose to revoke refresh tokens under certain conditions, such as when suspicious activity is detected, when a user changes their password, or when the user logs out of the application. By implementing token revocation policies, administrators can maintain tighter control over who has ongoing access to protected resources.

Another aspect of token lifecycles is token rotation. Token rotation involves issuing a new refresh token every time a client uses the current refresh token to obtain a new access token. This technique ensures that if a refresh token is compromised, it cannot be reused indefinitely. Once the authorization server issues a new refresh token, it invalidates the previous one. If an attacker attempts to use an old, invalidated refresh token, their request will fail. This strategy further enhances security by reducing the potential damage caused by a stolen refresh token.

The user experience is also a key consideration when defining token lifecycles. While short-lived tokens improve security, they can inconvenience users if they are frequently asked to reauthenticate. Refresh tokens help mitigate this by enabling clients to obtain new access tokens in the background, providing seamless access without constant interruptions. However, organizations must carefully balance security and convenience, ensuring that tokens remain short-lived enough to be secure while not overly burdening users. This balance can be achieved through thoughtful token expiration policies, secure storage practices, and regular security audits.

Exploring token lifecycles in depth allows organizations to fine-tune their OAuth 2.0 implementations, ensuring that tokens remain secure, manageable, and aligned with business goals. By carefully defining token lifespans, implementing rotation and revocation strategies, and continually monitoring token usage, organizations can maintain a secure authorization framework that meets both security and usability requirements.

Resource Owner Credentials Flow

The resource owner credentials flow, also known as the "password" grant type, is one of the grant types defined in the OAuth 2.0 specification. This flow allows a client application to directly obtain an access token by presenting the user's credentials—typically a username and password—to the authorization server. While it provides a straightforward method for obtaining tokens, it comes with significant security considerations and is generally recommended only in specific scenarios where other flows are not viable.

At a high level, the resource owner credentials flow involves the client collecting the resource owner's username and password and sending them directly to the authorization server. The authorization server verifies the credentials and, if they are valid, issues an access token that the client can use to access protected resources. This process bypasses the typical redirect-based flows that involve the resource owner interacting with a browser or user agent. Instead, the client acts on behalf of the resource owner, submitting their credentials directly and receiving a token in response.

The primary advantage of the resource owner credentials flow is its simplicity. By directly exchanging credentials for a token, it eliminates the need for additional steps such as redirections, consent screens, or authorization codes. This can be beneficial in scenarios where the client and resource owner have a high level of trust, and the client can be certain that the credentials will remain secure. For example, some internal applications or legacy systems might use this flow when other OAuth 2.0 flows are impractical or unsupported. In such cases, the resource owner credentials flow provides a straightforward path to obtaining access tokens without introducing the complexity of more indirect grant types.

Despite its simplicity, the resource owner credentials flow is not without drawbacks. The most significant concern is the direct handling of user credentials by the client. By collecting and transmitting the resource owner's password, the client assumes a higher level of responsibility for safeguarding sensitive information. If the client is compromised or if the credentials are intercepted, it can lead to unauthorized access to protected resources. Unlike other flows where the client never directly sees the user's password, this approach creates a point of vulnerability that must be carefully managed.

To mitigate these risks, the resource owner credentials flow should only be used in controlled environments where both the client and the resource owner are part of the same trusted entity. For instance, it might be acceptable in an organization's internal system where the client application is tightly controlled and resides within the company's secure network. In such cases, the client can be configured to securely store and transmit the credentials, reducing the likelihood of compromise. However, for third-party applications or public clients, this flow is strongly discouraged due to the inherent risk of exposing user credentials.

Another important consideration is that the resource owner credentials flow does not provide a mechanism for the resource owner to explicitly grant or revoke access on a per-client basis. Unlike other OAuth flows where the resource owner explicitly consents to a client's request for access, this flow relies on the client's ability to authenticate as the resource owner. This can limit the granularity of access control and make it harder to audit which clients have been granted access.

Organizations must carefully evaluate whether the simplicity of this flow outweighs the potential loss of fine-grained consent and control.

In addition to security concerns, the resource owner credentials flow may not align with modern authentication practices. Increasingly, organizations are adopting passwordless authentication methods, multi-factor authentication (MFA), and other advanced security measures that go beyond simple username-and-password credentials. The resource owner credentials flow, by its nature, is tied to traditional password-based authentication, which may conflict with these more secure approaches. As organizations move toward stronger authentication methods, they may find it necessary to transition away from the resource owner credentials flow in favor of other OAuth grant types that better support modern security requirements.

Despite these limitations, the resource owner credentials flow can be useful in certain controlled situations. For example, some legacy applications may not support the redirection-based flows that OAuth typically uses. In such cases, the resource owner credentials flow can serve as a bridge, allowing these older systems to integrate with an OAuth 2.0-based environment. By using this flow in a carefully controlled context, organizations can gradually modernize their authentication infrastructure without immediately replacing existing systems. Over time, as the infrastructure evolves, they can transition to more secure flows and reduce their reliance on direct credential handling.

Ultimately, the resource owner credentials flow is a tool that should be used with caution and in specific circumstances. While it offers simplicity and directness, it also introduces significant security and control challenges that must be carefully managed. Organizations should assess their unique requirements, consider the trust level between the client and resource owner, and weigh the risks before adopting this flow. In most cases, alternative grant types—such as the authorization code flow or client credentials flow—will provide a more secure and flexible solution for achieving delegated access.

Implicit Flow: Pros and Cons

The implicit flow, originally introduced in the OAuth 2.0 specification, was designed to accommodate clients that could not securely store secrets. It allowed single-page applications (SPAs) and certain mobile apps to obtain access tokens directly from the authorization server's authorization endpoint, bypassing the need for a back-channel server-to-server communication. By doing so, the implicit flow simplified the process of obtaining access tokens and eliminated the requirement for an intermediate authorization code. Despite these initial advantages, the flow has come under increasing scrutiny as the OAuth ecosystem has evolved, with both its benefits and drawbacks becoming clearer over time.

One of the main advantages of the implicit flow is its simplicity. By providing a direct path for obtaining an access token, the flow reduces the number of steps required to gain authorization. Once the resource owner grants permission, the authorization server immediately issues the access token, which the client can use right away. This streamlined approach made it particularly appealing for early SPAs and mobile apps, where the overhead of maintaining a secure backend component was often impractical or undesirable. Developers could focus on building their client-side logic without needing to implement additional server-side infrastructure, making it easier to integrate authentication into lightweight applications.

Another benefit of the implicit flow is that it eliminates the need for a client secret. Many public clients—such as JavaScript-based SPAs—cannot securely store secrets because their code is exposed to users. Since the implicit flow does not require a client secret, it avoids the risk of exposing this sensitive information in the client's codebase. This made it a suitable choice for environments where the lack of a secure storage mechanism for secrets was a given, and developers could still provide some level of authentication and access control.

Despite its simplicity, the implicit flow also introduces several notable challenges and security concerns. The most significant issue is the exposure of access tokens in the user-agent (e.g., the browser). Because the access token is included directly in the fragment of the redirect URI, it can be extracted from the browser history, intercepted by malicious browser extensions, or exposed through logs if the URI is captured in monitoring systems. These risks make the implicit flow inherently less secure than flows that obtain tokens through a back-channel exchange. If an access token is compromised, an attacker can potentially gain unauthorized access to protected resources for the duration of the token's validity.

Another drawback of the implicit flow is the lack of a refresh mechanism. Since the flow is designed to avoid client secrets and backend communication, it does not include refresh tokens. Once the access token expires, the user must re-authenticate, which can lead to a less seamless user experience. This limitation makes it more difficult to maintain long-term access without frequent interruptions. In contrast, flows that use a back-channel exchange can provide refresh tokens, allowing the client to request new access tokens silently, thus improving both usability and security.

The implicit flow also lacks some of the built-in security features present in more modern OAuth flows. For instance, the authorization code flow, when combined with Proof Key for Code Exchange (PKCE), provides an additional layer of security by requiring a client-generated code challenge and code verifier during the token exchange process. This ensures that even if an authorization code is intercepted, it cannot be used without the corresponding verifier. The implicit flow does not include these safeguards, making it more vulnerable to certain attacks, such as token injection or replay attacks, if the client's environment is not sufficiently secured.

The evolving OAuth 2.0 ecosystem has also contributed to the decline in the recommended use of the implicit flow. As best practices and security guidelines have matured, the industry has increasingly shifted toward using the authorization code flow with PKCE for public clients, including SPAs and mobile apps. PKCE eliminates the need for client secrets while still providing a secure token exchange process, effectively addressing the original challenges that the implicit flow sought to solve. This shift has reduced the reliance on the implicit flow and highlighted its inherent limitations.

Moreover, the implicit flow's security issues can be exacerbated in environments where the client application interacts with multiple resource servers or handles sensitive data. Since the access token is directly accessible in the client's runtime environment, it is more susceptible to exposure and misuse. As a result, organizations that prioritize security and compliance often avoid the implicit flow in favor of flows that provide more robust protection for tokens.

Despite these concerns, the implicit flow may still have a role in certain niche scenarios where the application's security requirements are relatively low, and simplicity is paramount. For example, in low-risk environments or for short-lived access to non-sensitive data, the implicit flow can offer a quick and easy way to implement OAuth 2.0 authentication. However, even in such cases, it is essential to carefully evaluate the potential risks and implement additional security measures, such as ensuring that the client's runtime environment is trusted and that the access token's lifespan is kept as short as possible.

The implicit flow has historically provided a convenient entry point for public clients needing a straightforward way to obtain access tokens. However, its inherent security trade-offs and the emergence of more secure alternatives have diminished its role in modern OAuth implementations. By understanding both its benefits and its limitations, organizations can make informed decisions about when— if ever—to use the implicit flow and when to adopt more secure and flexible authorization approaches.

Authorization Code Flow: The Industry Standard

The authorization code flow has become the de facto standard for securing OAuth 2.0 implementations, widely regarded as the most secure and flexible approach to obtaining tokens. This flow is specifically designed for confidential clients—applications that can securely store secrets on a server—and offers a robust framework for managing user authorization. By separating the user authentication step from the token exchange process, the authorization code flow minimizes the exposure of sensitive tokens and provides a higher level of protection against common attack vectors. As a result, it has gained widespread adoption in enterprise environments, SaaS platforms, and other use cases that demand a high level of security.

At a high level, the authorization code flow involves two distinct steps: first, the client application requests authorization from the resource owner (the user), and second, the client exchanges an authorization code for an access token. During the initial step, the user is redirected to the authorization server's authorization endpoint. The user authenticates, grants consent to the client application, and is then redirected back to the client with an authorization code. This code is a short-lived, single-use credential that cannot be used on its own to access resources. Instead, the client must send the code, along with its own credentials (client ID and client secret), to the authorization server's token endpoint to obtain an access token. By separating these steps, the authorization code flow ensures that the access token is never exposed in the user-agent (such as a browser), significantly reducing the risk of interception or misuse.

One of the key security benefits of the authorization code flow is that it allows the client application to maintain a back-channel communication with the authorization server. This means that sensitive credentials and tokens are exchanged securely between servers, rather than being exposed in the browser or on the client side. This back-channel exchange makes it more difficult for attackers to intercept tokens, as the communication is typically protected by HTTPS and is not accessible to the user's device or browser extensions. By keeping the token exchange out of the front-end environment, the authorization code flow provides a more secure foundation for building trusted applications and services.

The authorization code flow also supports a wide range of additional security measures, including Proof Key for Code Exchange (PKCE). PKCE was originally introduced to enhance the security of public clients, such as mobile apps or single-page applications (SPAs), that cannot securely store a client secret. With PKCE, the client generates a random code verifier and a corresponding code challenge before initiating the authorization request. The code challenge is sent to the authorization server along with the authorization request. When the client later exchanges the authorization code for an access token, it must include the code verifier. The authorization server checks that the code verifier matches the original challenge, ensuring that only the legitimate client can complete the token exchange. By adding PKCE to the authorization code flow, developers can extend its security benefits to public clients while maintaining the separation of the token exchange process from the user's browser or device.

Another advantage of the authorization code flow is its flexibility in integrating with various identity providers and authentication methods. Because the flow relies on the authorization server to handle authentication, it can easily incorporate multi-factor authentication (MFA), biometric authentication, or other advanced identity verification techniques. This makes the authorization code flow particularly well-suited for organizations that require strong, policy-driven authentication methods. Additionally, the flow's ability to handle complex user consent scenarios and attribute sharing makes it a preferred choice for applications that need to manage fine-grained access controls or comply with stringent regulatory requirements.

The widespread adoption of the authorization code flow is also a testament to its compatibility with modern application architectures. As organizations increasingly move toward microservices and API-first designs, the need for secure, reliable token issuance becomes critical. The authorization code flow's use of a dedicated token endpoint and back-channel communication aligns well with these distributed environments. Resource servers can validate access tokens issued through this flow, ensuring that only authorized requests are processed. Furthermore, the flow's support for refresh tokens allows clients to maintain long-lived sessions without repeatedly prompting the user for authentication, providing a smoother user experience and reducing the risk of session interruptions.

In practice, the authorization code flow has become the gold standard for OAuth 2.0 implementations. Its separation of user authentication from token issuance, support for advanced security features like PKCE, and ability to integrate with modern identity providers make it a versatile and secure choice. Organizations that adopt the authorization code flow benefit from a robust framework that protects sensitive credentials, mitigates risks, and provides the flexibility needed to meet diverse authentication and authorization requirements. As the identity and access management landscape continues to evolve, the authorization code flow remains the industry standard for building secure, scalable, and user-friendly OAuth 2.0 solutions.

Client Credentials Flow: Server-to-Server Authentication

The client credentials flow is a specialized OAuth 2.0 grant type designed for machine-to-machine authentication. Unlike other flows, it does not involve user authorization or resource owner approval. Instead, it enables a client—often a backend service, script, or application component—to directly authenticate with an authorization server using its own credentials. By issuing access tokens that grant limited, pre-defined permissions, the client credentials flow simplifies server-to-server communication while maintaining secure, controlled access to APIs and protected resources.

At the core of the client credentials flow is the concept of a "confidential client." A confidential client is a secure application or service that can safely store credentials, such as a client ID and client secret. These credentials are known only to the client and the authorization server, ensuring that they cannot be easily intercepted or misused. When the client needs to access a protected resource, it authenticates with the authorization server by presenting these credentials. If the credentials are valid, the authorization server issues an access token. The client then uses this token to make authorized requests to the resource server.

One of the key advantages of the client credentials flow is its simplicity. Since no user is involved, there is no need for redirection, consent prompts, or user-agent interactions. The client authenticates directly with the authorization server, and the entire process occurs through a server-to-server connection. This streamlined approach makes the client credentials flow ideal for non-interactive scenarios, such as backend APIs, automated processes, and microservices that need to authenticate to one another.

The flow also provides strong security by ensuring that only authorized clients can obtain access tokens. The client secret acts as a form of proof that the client is legitimate. When properly managed, the secret remains confidential and is never exposed to the end user or any public-facing environment. Additionally, the access tokens issued through the client credentials flow are typically short-lived and scoped.

This means they are valid only for a limited duration and grant access to specific resources or actions. If a token is compromised, its utility is restricted to the defined scope and expires quickly, reducing the potential for misuse.

Because the client credentials flow does not involve user authentication, it relies heavily on the configuration and policies set by the authorization server. The authorization server must enforce strict validation of the client credentials and ensure that each client is assigned appropriate scopes and permissions. For example, a client may be allowed to read data from a particular API endpoint but not modify it. By carefully defining these scopes, administrators maintain granular control over what each client can do, helping to minimize risks and prevent unauthorized operations.

Another advantage of the client credentials flow is its alignment with modern API-first architectures and microservices environments. As organizations shift toward distributed systems, many backend services need to interact with each other without user involvement. The client credentials flow provides a standardized method for these services to authenticate and obtain tokens that prove their identity and authorization level. This eliminates the need for custom authentication solutions and simplifies the process of managing credentials across multiple services.

The client credentials flow is also highly scalable. Since it does not depend on user interactions, it can handle high volumes of requests without introducing latency from user prompts or redirections. This makes it well-suited for scenarios where automated systems need to rapidly authenticate and access APIs. For example, an automated build pipeline might use the client credentials flow to retrieve deployment information from an API, or a monitoring system might authenticate to a metrics endpoint to gather performance data. In each case, the flow enables efficient, secure communication between services without human intervention.

While the client credentials flow offers many benefits, it also places significant responsibility on the client to protect its credentials. Confidential clients must implement best practices for credential storage and transmission. This includes using secure storage mechanisms, encrypting sensitive data, and ensuring that the client secret is never exposed in logs, environment variables, or source code. Additionally, organizations should regularly rotate client secrets and enforce strict access controls, limiting who can view or manage these credentials. By following these practices, clients can prevent credential leaks and maintain the integrity of the authentication process.

The client credentials flow is particularly useful in scenarios where no user is present to provide consent or authenticate directly. For instance, a billing system might need to retrieve data from a customer management API, or a data synchronization service might periodically update records in a remote database. In these cases, the flow's machine-to-machine authentication capabilities ensure that only authorized services can access the resources they need. This reduces the complexity of managing user-based permissions for tasks that do not involve human interaction.

The client credentials flow has become a cornerstone of server-to-server authentication in modern distributed systems. By providing a straightforward, secure mechanism for confidential clients to obtain access tokens, it enables seamless communication between backend services, APIs, and automated processes. Its simplicity, scalability, and alignment with microservices architectures make it a natural choice for many scenarios, helping organizations maintain secure, controlled access to their resources.

PKCE: Enhancing Security for Native Apps

Proof Key for Code Exchange (PKCE, pronounced "pixy") was introduced as an extension to the OAuth 2.0 authorization code flow to address security challenges commonly faced by native applications. Unlike confidential clients, which can securely store a client secret on a backend server, native apps—such as mobile apps or desktop applications—operate in environments where secrets can be easily exposed. PKCE enhances the security of these public clients by ensuring that even if an attacker intercepts the authorization code, they cannot exchange it for an access token without also possessing a unique, client-generated secret known as the code verifier.

At its core, PKCE modifies the standard authorization code flow by adding two key components: a code verifier and a code challenge. The code verifier is a random string generated by the client before making the authorization request. From this verifier, the client derives a code challenge, which is typically a hashed and base64-encoded version of the verifier. When the client initiates the authorization request, it includes the code challenge as an additional parameter. Once the user authenticates and the authorization server issues an authorization code, the client must present the original code verifier along with the code to obtain an access token. The authorization server compares the code verifier to the previously submitted code challenge to ensure they match. If they do not, the token request is rejected.

This additional step effectively mitigates the risk of code interception attacks. In the standard authorization code flow, if an attacker somehow captures the authorization code during the redirect back to the client—perhaps through a malicious browser extension, a compromised device, or a man-in-the-middle attack—they could potentially exchange that code for an access token. However, with PKCE in place, simply possessing the code is not enough. The attacker would also need the original code verifier, which is never transmitted to the authorization server until the final token exchange. Since the code verifier is kept secret by the client and only used internally, the attacker cannot complete the exchange, rendering the stolen code useless.

PKCE is particularly valuable in native app environments because these apps often run on devices that are inherently less secure than server environments. On mobile devices, for example, applications can be reverse-engineered, and any hardcoded secrets or tokens stored in the app package are at risk of exposure. Similarly, desktop applications run on operating systems where local users or malware may have access to memory or storage locations. In these scenarios, PKCE provides a layer of protection that does not rely on the ability to securely store a client secret. By binding the authorization code to the code verifier, PKCE ensures that only the legitimate instance of the client that generated the verifier can complete the flow.

Another important aspect of PKCE is that it does not require any changes to the user experience or the basic OAuth 2.0 flow. Users still authenticate through the authorization server's user interface, and the overall process remains familiar to developers and end-users. The security enhancements are implemented entirely on the client and authorization server side, making PKCE a seamless addition to existing OAuth integrations. For developers, this means they can adopt PKCE without needing to redesign their authentication flow or introduce significant complexity into their codebase.

PKCE also aligns well with modern security practices and complements other security mechanisms. While it primarily protects against interception of the authorization code, it works in tandem with TLS (Transport Layer Security) to ensure that all communications between the client and the authorization server are encrypted. Additionally, by leveraging best practices for random string generation and secure hashing algorithms (such as SHA-256), PKCE strengthens the overall security posture of the authorization process. These layered defenses make it significantly more difficult for attackers to exploit vulnerabilities in the authorization code flow.

Although PKCE was originally developed to address the needs of native apps, it has become a best practice for any OAuth 2.0 implementation that uses the authorization code flow. Public clients, single-page applications (SPAs), and other environments where a client secret cannot be securely stored benefit greatly from the enhanced protection PKCE provides. In fact, the OAuth working group recommends using PKCE whenever possible, even for confidential clients, as it provides an extra layer of defense against potential code interception. By making PKCE a standard part of their OAuth implementations, developers can ensure a more robust and secure authorization process, regardless of the client's environment.

OAuth 2.0 Scopes and Permissions

Scopes and permissions are fundamental to the OAuth 2.0 authorization framework, serving as a way to define and control the level of access that a client application has to a user's resources. By explicitly stating what the client is allowed to do and which resources it can access, scopes help ensure that the principle of least privilege is maintained. This allows for fine-grained control, giving resource owners confidence that their data is only accessible to the extent necessary and only to trusted parties. Understanding how scopes and permissions work is essential for building secure and user-friendly OAuth 2.0 implementations.

A scope in OAuth 2.0 is a string that represents a specific level of access to a resource or a certain action that can be performed. For example, a social media API might define a scope for reading a user's profile information, another scope for posting on their behalf, and yet another for accessing their private messages. When a client application requests authorization, it includes a list of scopes that it wants the user to approve. This allows the user to see, in clear terms, what actions the application intends to perform. If the user consents, the authorization server issues an access token with those scopes attached. The resource server then uses the scopes to determine whether the client's requests are permitted.

Scopes not only improve security by limiting what a client can do, but they also enhance transparency and trust. When users can see exactly what an application is requesting—such as "read your contacts" or "write to your calendar"—they are more likely to feel comfortable granting access. Without scopes, a client might gain broad, undefined permissions, leading users to distrust the process or hesitate to grant authorization. Scopes provide a clear, bounded set of permissions, ensuring that users remain in control of their data.

Permissions, on the other hand, are often used interchangeably with scopes but can also refer to the internal rules and roles that govern access to resources. While scopes define what the client can request from the resource owner, permissions typically refer to the policies enforced by the resource server. For example, a user may have permissions based on their role—such as "admin" or "editor"—that determine what data they can access or modify. When an access token is presented, the resource server checks both the scopes included in the token and the user's underlying permissions to make a final access control decision. In this way, scopes and permissions work together: scopes limit what the client can request, while permissions ensure that only authorized actions are actually performed.

The process of requesting and granting scopes is an interactive one. When the client application redirects the user to the authorization server's consent page, it includes the desired scopes as part of the request. The authorization server then presents these scopes to the user, allowing them to review the requested permissions before granting or denying access. This transparent, user-driven approval process is one of the key security and usability features of OAuth 2.0. By putting the user in control, OAuth builds trust and ensures that access is only granted with informed consent.

Once the access token is issued, it serves as proof that the user has consented to the specified scopes. Each request that the client makes to the resource server includes this token. The resource server extracts the scopes from the token and compares them against the requested operation. If the token includes the necessary scope—for example, "read:user_profile" for retrieving profile data—the request is allowed. If not, the resource server rejects the request, maintaining strict access control.

From a developer's perspective, defining appropriate scopes is a crucial design consideration. If the scopes are too broad, clients may end up with more access than they need, increasing the risk of data misuse. If the scopes are too granular, the user experience can become cumbersome, with users needing to approve numerous small permissions. Striking the right balance requires a clear understanding of the application's functionality and the sensitivity of the data involved. By carefully designing scopes, developers can ensure that clients request only what they need, reducing the risk of over-privileged tokens and improving user trust.

Another important aspect is the ability to introduce new scopes or modify existing ones over time. As APIs evolve, new features may require additional levels of access. The OAuth framework supports this by allowing developers to define new scopes and integrate them into the authorization process. However, when introducing new scopes, it's critical to ensure backward compatibility and communicate changes to both developers and users. By carefully managing scope evolution, organizations can maintain secure, transparent access while keeping pace with new requirements and functionality.

In distributed and microservices-based architectures, scopes become even more valuable. As different services expose their own sets of APIs, scopes help define clear boundaries around what each client can access. For example, a single access token might carry multiple scopes, such as "read:user_profile" and "read:purchase_history," each corresponding to a different microservice. This fine-grained approach to access control allows organizations to maintain security across a complex environment, ensuring that each component of the system enforces appropriate boundaries.

The Role of the Authorization Server

The authorization server plays a central role in the OAuth 2.0 framework, serving as the trusted authority that handles user authentication, manages consent, and issues tokens. By acting as the intermediary between clients, resource owners, and resource servers, the authorization server ensures that only authorized clients gain access to protected resources. Its responsibilities encompass authenticating users, validating client credentials, enforcing policies, and ultimately issuing the access and refresh tokens that clients use to interact securely with APIs. Understanding the role and operation of the authorization server is essential for designing secure, reliable OAuth 2.0 implementations.

One of the primary functions of the authorization server is to authenticate the resource owner. When a user initiates the authorization process, the authorization server prompts them to log in and prove their identity. This authentication step can take many forms, from simple username-and-password combinations to multi-factor authentication (MFA) or biometrics. By verifying the user's identity, the authorization server lays the foundation for a secure, trusted interaction between the user, the client application, and the protected resources. Authentication is the first critical step in ensuring that only legitimate resource owners can grant access to their data.

After authenticating the user, the authorization server handles user consent. Before issuing tokens, it presents the user with a consent screen that outlines what the client application is requesting. This might include specific scopes, such as reading the user's profile information, posting on their behalf, or accessing certain data sets. The user must explicitly approve or deny these requests. By requiring consent, the authorization server provides transparency and gives the resource owner control over their data. Users can review and make informed decisions about what they're allowing, which helps build trust and ensures compliance with privacy regulations.

Once the user grants consent, the authorization server is responsible for issuing tokens. These tokens—such as access tokens and refresh tokens—serve as credentials that the client application uses to interact with resource servers. The authorization server generates these tokens in accordance with the client's request and the user's consent. Access tokens are typically short-lived, limiting the window during which they can be used, while refresh tokens allow clients to maintain a session without requiring the user to log in again. By issuing tokens with defined scopes and expiration times, the authorization server ensures that access is controlled, time-bound, and aligned with the user's preferences.

Another critical role of the authorization server is validating client credentials. In addition to authenticating users, it also verifies the identity of the client application. For confidential clients—those that can securely store secrets—the authorization server checks the client's ID and secret. For public clients—such as single-page applications or mobile apps—it may rely on other security mechanisms like Proof Key for Code Exchange (PKCE). This validation step ensures that only trusted clients can request tokens, protecting the resource owner's data from unauthorized or malicious applications.

The authorization server also enforces policies and compliance requirements. Organizations often define policies around who can access certain resources, under what conditions, and for how long. The authorization server enforces these rules, ensuring that tokens are issued only under acceptable circumstances. For example, it might require MFA for sensitive operations, limit token lifetimes for high-risk clients, or deny requests from clients that do not meet certain security standards. By embedding these policies into the authorization process, the authorization server helps maintain compliance with industry regulations, corporate policies, and security best practices.

Another important function of the authorization server is maintaining logs and audit trails. Every authorization request, authentication event, and token issuance is recorded. These logs provide valuable insights into who accessed which resources, when, and for how long. In the event of a security incident or audit, these records allow administrators to trace the origin of access, identify unusual patterns, and take corrective action. The authorization server's logging capabilities are essential for maintaining accountability and ensuring that the entire OAuth 2.0 environment remains secure and transparent.

In addition to these core responsibilities, the authorization server often integrates with external identity providers and directories. Many organizations use existing identity sources—such as Active Directory, LDAP, or a social login provider—to authenticate users. The authorization server can act as a bridge, connecting these identity providers to the OAuth ecosystem. By leveraging existing authentication infrastructure, the authorization server ensures consistency and simplifies user management, while still providing the benefits of token-based access control.

The authorization server's role extends beyond simply issuing tokens; it sets the foundation for secure, controlled interactions between all parties in the OAuth 2.0 framework. It authenticates users, validates clients, enforces policies, manages consent, and provides a central point for logging and compliance. By carefully configuring and managing the authorization server, organizations can maintain a secure, scalable, and user-friendly identity and access management environment.

How Resource Servers Validate Tokens

In the OAuth 2.0 framework, the resource server plays a critical role in ensuring that access tokens presented by clients are valid, authentic, and authorized. By performing token validation, the resource server can reliably determine whether a given request should be permitted or denied. This process involves several key steps, including verifying the token's integrity, checking its scope, ensuring it hasn't expired, and confirming that it comes from a trusted authorization server. Through careful validation, resource servers help maintain the security of protected resources and prevent unauthorized access.

The first and most fundamental step in token validation is ensuring the token's integrity and authenticity. Many OAuth 2.0 implementations use JSON Web Tokens (JWTs) as access tokens. A JWT is a compact, self-contained token format that includes claims about the resource owner, the client, and the permissions granted. JWTs are digitally signed by the authorization server using a private key. When the resource server receives a JWT, it uses the corresponding public key to verify the signature. If the signature is valid, it confirms that the token was issued by the trusted authorization server and has not been tampered with. If the signature verification fails, the resource server rejects the token outright, preventing any further processing.

In some scenarios, access tokens are not JWTs but rather opaque tokens. Unlike JWTs, opaque tokens do not contain readable claims or signatures that can be verified directly. Instead, the resource server must rely on an external introspection endpoint provided by the authorization server. When a client presents an opaque token, the resource server sends it to the introspection endpoint. The authorization server responds with metadata about the token, including whether it is active, what scopes it includes, and when it expires. Based on this information, the resource server can make an informed decision about whether to allow the request. While this approach requires an additional network call, it ensures that the resource server always has the most up-to-date information about the token's validity.

Token expiration is another critical factor in validation. Access tokens are typically short-lived, with expiration times set by the authorization server. The resource server must check the token's "exp" claim (in the case of a JWT) or the expiration data returned from the introspection endpoint. If the current time is beyond the token's expiration time, the token is considered invalid and the request is denied. By enforcing token expiration, resource servers limit the window of opportunity for an attacker to use a stolen token, reducing the potential for abuse.

Scopes are a key component of token validation, as they define what the client is allowed to do. When a token is issued, it includes a set of scopes that specify the actions and resources the client can access. The resource server must check these scopes against the requested operation. For example, if a token includes a "read:profile" scope but the client tries to update user information, the resource server should deny the request. This ensures that even if a client possesses a valid token, it cannot perform actions beyond what was originally authorized. By enforcing scope checks, resource servers maintain strict access control and prevent privilege escalation.

The resource server must also confirm that the token comes from a trusted source. This involves verifying the issuer claim in a JWT or ensuring that the introspection endpoint is provided by a known, trusted authorization server. In multi-tenant environments or federated scenarios, the resource server may need to validate tokens issued by multiple authorization servers. In such cases, the resource server maintains a list of trusted issuers or public keys. If a token's issuer is not on the trusted list, the token is rejected. This process helps prevent unauthorized tokens from rogue or untrusted authorization servers from gaining access to protected resources.

Another layer of validation involves token revocation. Although access tokens are typically short-lived, there may be scenarios where an active token needs to be invalidated before it expires. For example, if a user revokes consent, changes their password, or if the token is suspected to be compromised, the authorization server can mark it as no longer valid. In some implementations, the resource server can query a revocation endpoint or cache a list of revoked tokens. If the presented token matches a revoked token, the resource server denies the request. By incorporating revocation checks, resource servers can enforce real-time security measures, preventing further access even if the token was previously valid.

Logging and auditing also play a crucial role in token validation. Every time the resource server validates a token, it can record information such as the token's issuer, expiration time, scopes, and the client that presented it. These logs provide valuable insights into token usage patterns, help identify potential misuse, and assist in troubleshooting authentication issues. Additionally, maintaining detailed logs supports compliance and audit requirements, ensuring that resource servers uphold organizational security policies and regulatory standards.

Overall, token validation by the resource server is a multi-step process that encompasses verifying signatures, checking scopes, enforcing expiration, confirming the issuer, and handling revocations. By diligently performing these validations, resource servers ensure that only authorized clients gain access to protected resources, maintaining the integrity and security of the entire OAuth 2.0 ecosystem.

OpenID Connect and OAuth 2.0

OpenID Connect (OIDC) builds on the OAuth 2.0 framework to provide a simple and standardized way to perform user authentication and obtain basic profile information. While OAuth 2.0 was originally designed as a delegation protocol to grant third-party applications limited access to resources, it does not define how to authenticate users or retrieve their identity information. OpenID Connect fills this gap by adding an identity layer on top of OAuth 2.0, offering a unified method for logging in users and obtaining verified claims about them. By integrating authentication and authorization, OpenID Connect enables developers to implement secure and user-friendly login experiences across diverse platforms and applications.

One of the key elements introduced by OpenID Connect is the ID token. The ID token is a JSON Web Token (JWT) that contains identity claims about the authenticated user. These claims typically include information such as the user's unique identifier (sub), name, email address, and any other attributes that the OpenID provider (OP) is configured to return. The ID token is digitally signed by the OP, allowing the client to verify its authenticity without making additional network calls. This self-contained nature makes it efficient for clients to quickly validate the user's identity and extract relevant information.

The OpenID Connect protocol relies heavily on the OAuth 2.0 authorization code flow, but it modifies and extends the flow to support authentication. When a user logs in, the client redirects the user to the OpenID provider's authorization endpoint, just as it would in a standard OAuth flow. The user authenticates and grants consent to share their information. Once the OP completes authentication, it redirects the user back to the client with an authorization code. The client then exchanges this code at the token endpoint to obtain both an access token (for resource authorization) and an ID token (for authentication). By combining these tokens, OpenID Connect allows the client to perform both authentication and resource access control in a seamless manner.

OpenID Connect also introduces the concept of discovery and dynamic registration. The OpenID Connect Discovery specification defines a well-known configuration endpoint that clients can query to retrieve information about the OP's endpoints, supported scopes, and public keys. This simplifies the integration process, as developers no longer need to manually configure endpoint URLs or keys. Dynamic registration allows clients to register with the OP at runtime, further streamlining setup and reducing the manual steps required to onboard new applications. Together, these features enhance interoperability and make OpenID Connect easy to implement across various environments.

Another significant advantage of OpenID Connect is its compatibility with a wide range of modern application types. Single-page applications (SPAs), mobile apps, and server-side web applications can all use OpenID Connect to authenticate users and obtain identity claims. The protocol's flexibility means that developers can rely on a consistent approach regardless of the platform. For SPAs, OpenID Connect can be combined with Proof Key for Code Exchange (PKCE) to ensure secure token exchanges. Mobile applications can use native browser-based flows to perform authentication, and server-side apps can securely store client secrets and manage long-term sessions. This versatility makes OpenID Connect an attractive choice for developers building cross-platform solutions.

In addition to basic authentication, OpenID Connect supports advanced scenarios through its optional specifications and extensions. The OpenID Connect Session Management and Front-Channel Logout specifications provide mechanisms for maintaining consistent session state and performing coordinated logouts across multiple clients. The OpenID Connect Back-Channel Logout spec allows the OP to notify clients about logout events without requiring direct user interaction. These features help ensure a seamless user experience, particularly in environments where multiple applications are tied to a single user session.

Security is a cornerstone of OpenID Connect. The protocol incorporates best practices from OAuth 2.0, such as requiring secure TLS connections and leveraging JWT signatures to protect token integrity. Additionally, OpenID Connect emphasizes the importance of audience restrictions and issuer verification. Clients must validate that the ID token's issuer matches the expected OP and that the token is intended for the client's audience. These validation steps prevent tokens from being reused or accepted by unintended parties, reinforcing the protocol's security guarantees.

OpenID Connect also introduces the "nonce" parameter to protect against replay attacks. When initiating an authentication request, the client includes a randomly generated nonce. This value is echoed back in the ID token's payload. Upon receiving the token, the client verifies that the nonce matches what it initially sent. If it doesn't, the token is rejected. This mechanism ensures that each authentication request is unique and that a malicious actor cannot reuse an intercepted response.

By building on OAuth 2.0 and introducing a standardized way to handle authentication, OpenID Connect has become a widely adopted protocol for modern identity solutions. It simplifies the process of integrating user authentication into applications, provides verified user claims through the ID token, and ensures secure token exchanges through best practices and extensions. Its flexibility, ease of integration, and robust security model have made OpenID Connect a cornerstone of many identity and access management systems, enabling developers to deliver secure and seamless authentication experiences.

Token Revocation and Introspection

Token revocation and introspection are key components of managing OAuth 2.0 access and refresh tokens. These processes allow authorization servers and resource servers to enforce fine-grained control over token lifecycles, ensuring that tokens can be invalidated or verified in real time. By leveraging revocation endpoints and introspection mechanisms, administrators can maintain a higher level of security, quickly respond to security incidents, and reduce the risk of unauthorized access to protected resources.

Token revocation provides a standardized method for invalidating tokens before their natural expiration. In many OAuth 2.0 implementations, tokens are issued with a fixed lifetime. While this limited lifespan helps reduce risk, there are scenarios where tokens must be immediately invalidated. For example, if a user changes their password, revokes an application's access, or reports that their credentials have been compromised, the associated tokens should be rendered invalid as soon as possible. The OAuth 2.0 Token Revocation specification introduces a revocation endpoint, which clients or administrators can call to signal that a token is no longer valid. Once revoked, any subsequent attempt to use the token for authentication or authorization fails, effectively cutting off access.

Revocation is particularly useful in multi-device or multi-session environments. Imagine a user who is logged in on multiple devices and loses one of them. By revoking the token associated with the lost device, the authorization server can ensure that access from that device is blocked without affecting the other active sessions. This approach provides flexibility and precision, allowing administrators to maintain security without disrupting valid, ongoing sessions.

In addition to revocation, token introspection is a powerful tool that allows resource servers to verify the status and validity of a token in real time. Instead of relying solely on static token expiration or signature verification, introspection enables dynamic checks against the authorization server. The OAuth 2.0 Token Introspection specification defines a standard endpoint that resource servers can call to obtain metadata about a token. When the resource server receives a token from a client, it sends the token to the introspection endpoint and receives a response containing details such as whether the token is active, which scopes it was granted, who issued it, and when it expires. This real-time validation adds an extra layer of assurance, particularly in environments where tokens may be revoked or where additional runtime checks are required.

Token introspection is especially valuable in distributed systems and federated environments. In a microservices architecture, for example, multiple resource servers may need to handle requests from the same set of tokens. Instead of each server maintaining its own token validation logic or key storage, they can rely on a central introspection endpoint. This approach simplifies token management and ensures consistency across the system. If a token is revoked or modified, all resource servers can immediately detect the change and deny access accordingly.

Combining revocation and introspection provides a comprehensive approach to token lifecycle management. Revocation ensures that tokens can be invalidated proactively, while introspection allows for dynamic, real-time validation. Together, these capabilities give administrators greater control over how and when tokens are used. For instance, if a client application is found to be misbehaving, administrators can revoke its tokens and rely on introspection to enforce that revocation across all resource servers. Similarly, if a compliance policy requires frequent token status checks, introspection allows resource servers to confirm that tokens are still valid before granting access.

Implementing token revocation and introspection requires careful consideration of performance and scalability. Since introspection involves network calls to the authorization server, excessive reliance on it can introduce latency and impact the responsiveness of resource servers. To mitigate this, organizations can adopt caching strategies. For example, resource servers might cache positive introspection responses for a short period, reducing the number of calls to the introspection endpoint while still ensuring timely updates. Similarly, revocation events can be propagated to resource servers through pub/sub mechanisms or push notifications, allowing them to update their cached token state without making repeated introspection calls. Balancing these approaches helps maintain a high level of security without sacrificing performance.

Another consideration is the level of detail returned by the introspection endpoint. Depending on the environment and the sensitivity of the data involved, the introspection response may include additional claims, roles, or attributes about the token's subject. This information can help resource servers make more informed access control decisions. However, it is crucial to secure the introspection endpoint itself, ensuring that only authorized resource servers and administrators can call it. By limiting access and using strong authentication methods for the introspection endpoint, organizations can prevent unauthorized parties from obtaining sensitive token metadata.

Overall, token revocation and introspection are essential tools in modern OAuth 2.0 deployments. By allowing administrators to immediately invalidate tokens and resource servers to verify tokens dynamically, these processes enhance security, improve compliance, and ensure that token-based access remains tightly controlled. Integrating both revocation and introspection into an OAuth 2.0 architecture provides a robust, flexible approach to managing tokens, enabling organizations to maintain secure and scalable authorization frameworks.

Protecting APIs with OAuth 2.0

As APIs have become the backbone of modern applications and services, ensuring their security has become a critical priority. OAuth 2.0 offers a comprehensive framework for securing APIs, providing a flexible and standardized approach to controlling access. By leveraging OAuth 2.0, API providers can enforce fine-grained permissions, authenticate clients without relying on passwords, and limit the scope of what each application can do. Through the use of access tokens, refresh tokens, scopes, and robust authorization flows, OAuth 2.0 helps developers protect sensitive data, prevent unauthorized access, and maintain trust between clients and the APIs they consume.

At the heart of OAuth 2.0's approach to API security is the concept of access tokens. Access tokens serve as digital credentials that clients present when making requests to protected endpoints. Instead of sharing a user's credentials directly, clients obtain tokens through an authorization flow and use them to access APIs on behalf of the user. These tokens are typically short-lived, reducing the impact of a token falling into the wrong hands. By verifying the token before processing a request, the API ensures that only authorized clients can perform specific operations, effectively safeguarding resources.

Scopes further enhance security by limiting what clients can do with the tokens they receive. A scope defines a specific level of access or a particular set of actions that a token permits. For instance, an API that manages user data might define separate scopes for reading user profiles, writing to their accounts, and deleting their data. When a client requests authorization, it specifies which scopes it needs. The resource owner can review these scopes and decide whether to grant them. By enforcing scope checks at the API level, developers can ensure that even if a token is valid, it cannot be used to perform unauthorized actions. This principle of least privilege helps reduce the attack surface and ensures that clients only have the permissions they truly need.

Another critical component of protecting APIs with OAuth 2.0 is the proper implementation of authorization flows. Different flows, such as the authorization code flow, implicit flow, and client credentials flow, cater to various scenarios. For instance, server-based applications that can securely store secrets typically use the authorization code flow, which provides a high level of security. Public clients, like single-page applications or mobile apps, can leverage the authorization code flow with Proof Key for Code Exchange (PKCE) to mitigate the risk of code interception. Machine-to-machine communications often rely on the client credentials flow, allowing backend services to authenticate without involving a user. By selecting the appropriate flow for each use case, developers ensure that API access is granted securely, with minimal risk of compromise.

Token validation is a key part of protecting APIs with OAuth 2.0. Before processing any request, the API checks whether the presented token is valid, unexpired, and correctly scoped. Many APIs use JSON Web Tokens (JWTs) as access tokens, which can be verified locally without additional network calls. This approach reduces latency and improves performance while still ensuring token integrity. If the token is not a JWT or additional checks are required, the API may query an introspection endpoint provided by the authorization server. This endpoint confirms whether the token is still active, what scopes it contains, and when it expires. By performing these validation steps, the API ensures that only legitimate, authorized requests are fulfilled.

The revocation of tokens also plays a crucial role in API protection. If a user revokes access for a particular client, or if a token is suspected to be compromised, the authorization server can mark the token as invalid. APIs should respect these revocation events and deny further access attempts using the revoked token. Some implementations use caching or subscription models to stay informed about revoked tokens in real time, ensuring that the API can respond quickly to changes in token validity. This proactive approach helps maintain a secure environment even in the face of changing access conditions.

OAuth 2.0 also supports the use of refresh tokens, which allow clients to obtain new access tokens without requiring the user to reauthenticate. While refresh tokens improve the user experience by enabling seamless session continuity, they must be handled carefully to maintain security. APIs and authorization servers often set strict policies around refresh token lifetimes, rotation, and storage. If a refresh token is compromised, it should be promptly revoked to prevent unauthorized access. By using refresh tokens wisely, developers can balance convenience and security, ensuring that APIs remain protected while delivering a smooth user experience.

API gateways and middleware further enhance OAuth 2.0's protective capabilities. Many organizations deploy API gateways to centralize authentication, authorization, and rate limiting. These gateways integrate with OAuth 2.0 to validate tokens, enforce scopes, and ensure that only authorized clients can access specific endpoints. By offloading much of the token validation and authorization logic to the gateway, developers can streamline API code and focus on business logic. This approach also simplifies the enforcement of consistent security policies across multiple APIs, reducing the risk of inconsistent implementations and gaps in protection.

In addition to these technical measures, monitoring and logging are essential for maintaining a secure API environment. APIs protected with OAuth 2.0 should log authentication attempts, token validations, and scope checks. These logs provide valuable insights into usage patterns and potential security issues. By analyzing logs, developers can identify unusual activity, detect potential breaches, and respond quickly to emerging threats. Coupled with regular security reviews and audits, these practices help ensure that OAuth 2.0 implementations remain robust, up-to-date, and effective in protecting APIs from unauthorized access and abuse.

OAuth 2.0 vs. OAuth 1.0

OAuth 2.0 and OAuth 1.0 are both protocols designed to enable secure authorization, but they differ significantly in terms of complexity, implementation details, and flexibility. OAuth 1.0, introduced in 2007, was the original specification that provided a way for third-party applications to access resources on behalf of a user without requiring the user's password. While it was groundbreaking at the time, OAuth 1.0's reliance on cryptographic signing, multiple token types, and complex workflows made it challenging for developers to implement and maintain. OAuth 2.0, released in 2012, sought to address these challenges by simplifying the architecture, reducing the burden on developers, and increasing the protocol's extensibility.

One of the most notable differences between OAuth 1.0 and OAuth 2.0 is the approach to securing requests. OAuth 1.0 relies heavily on signature-based security. Each request must be signed using a shared secret and a signature method, such as HMAC-SHA1. This requires developers to carefully construct the signature base string, normalize parameters, and ensure that every API call is signed correctly. While this approach provides strong security, it introduces significant complexity. Even small mistakes in parameter encoding or signature generation can cause authorization failures, leading to a steep learning curve for developers. In contrast, OAuth 2.0 abandons signature-based security in favor of relying on HTTPS to protect communications. By requiring that all interactions occur over secure channels, OAuth 2.0 simplifies the developer's task. Developers no longer need to manage cryptographic signing directly, which reduces implementation errors and speeds up development.

Another key difference is the use of tokens. OAuth 1.0 uses two types of tokens: request tokens and access tokens. The request token is a temporary token obtained from the service provider's API before the user authorizes the application. After the user grants permission, the request token is exchanged for an access token, which the application then uses to access protected resources. This two-step process is more complex and can be confusing for developers. OAuth 2.0 streamlines this process by eliminating the request token. Instead, it introduces a single authorization code that the application uses to obtain an access token. This simplification reduces the number of steps required, making it easier for developers to implement the protocol.

OAuth 2.0 also introduces a more flexible and modular approach to handling different types of clients and use cases. OAuth 1.0 treats all clients similarly, regardless of whether they are server-based applications, browser-based apps, or mobile apps. This lack of differentiation can lead to security challenges when adapting the protocol to diverse environments. OAuth 2.0 addresses this by defining multiple grant types, each tailored to a specific scenario. The authorization code grant is designed for server-based applications that can securely store secrets. The implicit grant is intended for single-page applications that cannot keep secrets secure. The client credentials grant is used for machine-to-machine communication, and the resource owner password credentials grant is for legacy scenarios where other flows are not feasible. By offering different grants, OAuth 2.0 provides developers with a more flexible framework that better fits their specific needs.

Extensibility is another area where OAuth 2.0 outshines OAuth 1.0. The original OAuth 1.0 specification was relatively rigid, leaving little room for customization or the addition of new features. OAuth 2.0, on the other hand, was designed with extensibility in mind. The specification outlines a core framework but allows for additional extensions and profiles. For example, OpenID Connect builds on OAuth 2.0 to provide an identity layer that handles user authentication. Other extensions introduce token introspection, token revocation, and additional security mechanisms like Proof Key for Code Exchange (PKCE). This extensibility ensures that OAuth 2.0 can evolve over time, adapting to new requirements and security challenges without breaking existing implementations.

One of the challenges with OAuth 1.0 was its lack of standardization around resource owner authentication. OAuth 1.0 left the details of user authentication largely up to the service provider. This led to inconsistent implementations and a lack of interoperability between different OAuth providers. OAuth 2.0, while still not specifying a single authentication method, provides clearer guidelines and works more seamlessly with standardized identity providers and authentication protocols. The introduction of OpenID Connect as a standardized identity layer further enhances interoperability, allowing developers to integrate user authentication more easily into their applications.

Despite the improvements in OAuth 2.0, it's worth noting that the shift to a simpler framework came with trade-offs. The reliance on HTTPS for securing communications means that OAuth 2.0 implementers must ensure proper TLS configurations and certificate management. While this is generally considered a best practice, it places greater importance on the underlying transport security. In contrast, OAuth 1.0's signature-based approach provided an additional layer of cryptographic security that was independent of transport. However, the simplicity and developer-friendly nature of OAuth 2.0 have made it the more widely adopted standard, as most organizations find the reduced complexity outweighs the trade-offs.

In summary, OAuth 2.0 represents a significant evolution over OAuth 1.0. By simplifying the security model, introducing flexible grant types, and providing a more extensible framework, OAuth 2.0 has become the industry standard for secure authorization. While OAuth 1.0 paved the way and demonstrated the need for a standardized approach to third-party access, OAuth 2.0's enhancements have made it easier for developers to implement, maintain, and adapt their authorization systems to meet modern requirements.

The Evolution of OAuth Standards

OAuth has come a long way since its inception, evolving from a niche solution for delegating access into a foundational standard for secure authorization and authentication on the modern web. Over the years, the protocol has undergone significant changes, addressing both the limitations of its early implementations and the shifting requirements of an increasingly connected, mobile-first digital landscape. By examining the progression from OAuth 1.0 to OAuth 2.0 and beyond, we can better understand how the standard has adapted to new challenges, improved security, and expanded its scope to meet the needs of developers and users alike.

The origins of OAuth date back to the mid-2000s, when developers sought a more secure and standardized method for third-party applications to access user resources. Before OAuth, applications often asked users for their account credentials, stored them locally, and used them to authenticate API requests. This approach presented numerous security risks. If a third-party app's database was compromised, attackers could gain access to the user's credentials and, by extension, all of the user's data on the associated service. Furthermore, users had no way to grant limited permissions; once an application had their credentials, it had unrestricted access. OAuth emerged as a solution to this problem, enabling users to delegate access to their resources without exposing their credentials to third-party apps.

The first major milestone in OAuth's evolution was the release of OAuth 1.0 in 2007. The original specification introduced the concept of access tokens, which allowed applications to act on a user's behalf without needing their password. Instead of sharing credentials, users would grant an application permission via a separate authorization step, after which the application would receive an access token. This token could then be used to make authorized API requests. While OAuth 1.0 represented a significant step forward, it was not without challenges. Its reliance on complex cryptographic signatures, a multi-step token exchange process, and strict parameter encoding rules made it difficult for developers to implement. Many found the protocol cumbersome and prone to errors, particularly for those new to cryptography or unfamiliar with the nuances of the specification.

In 2012, the introduction of OAuth 2.0 marked a turning point in the protocol's evolution. OAuth 2.0 was designed to simplify implementation, improve scalability, and provide greater flexibility for diverse use cases. One of the most significant changes was the removal of cryptographic signing from the core specification. Instead of requiring every request to be signed, OAuth 2.0 relies on HTTPS to secure communications. By offloading security to the transport layer, the protocol became much easier to implement, making it more accessible to developers with varying levels of expertise. This simplification, combined with more modular and extensible design principles, allowed OAuth 2.0 to gain widespread adoption across a broad range of applications, from mobile apps to enterprise APIs.

OAuth 2.0 also introduced new grant types to accommodate different types of clients and workflows. The authorization code flow provided a secure way for server-side applications to obtain tokens, while the implicit flow offered a lightweight solution for single-page applications. The client credentials flow enabled machine-to-machine communication, and the resource owner password credentials flow addressed scenarios where users trusted the client enough to provide their credentials directly. These grant types expanded OAuth's applicability, making it suitable for everything from consumer-facing apps to complex microservices architectures.

Despite its strengths, OAuth 2.0 was not immune to criticism. Some security experts expressed concern over the protocol's reliance on HTTPS alone, arguing that the removal of signature-based protections reduced resilience against certain attack vectors. In response to these concerns, the OAuth community continued to refine and extend the protocol through additional specifications and best practices. Proof Key for Code Exchange (PKCE), for example, was introduced to enhance the security of public clients—such as mobile apps and single-page applications—by adding a verifier and challenge mechanism to the authorization code flow. This mitigated the risk of code interception attacks, strengthening OAuth's security model in environments where secrets could not be securely stored.

The OAuth standard has also evolved to support new use cases and technologies. For instance, the introduction of token introspection and revocation endpoints allowed resource servers to verify token validity and respond to real-time security events. The development of the JSON Web Token (JWT) specification provided a standardized token format that is compact, self-contained, and easily verifiable, enabling faster and more efficient token validation. These advancements have made OAuth a more flexible and robust solution for modern authentication and authorization needs.

In addition to addressing security and usability challenges, OAuth's evolution has been driven by the growing demand for interoperability and user-centric identity solutions. OpenID Connect, built on top of OAuth 2.0, introduced a standardized way to handle user authentication and retrieve identity claims. By combining the delegation model of OAuth with a straightforward, developer-friendly approach to user login, OpenID Connect opened the door for widespread adoption by identity providers, social login platforms, and federated identity systems. This integration further solidified OAuth's position as the cornerstone of modern identity and access management.

The evolution of OAuth has been shaped not only by technological advancements but also by the active and collaborative efforts of the developer community. Working groups, open-source implementations, and industry stakeholders have all contributed to the standard's refinement, ensuring that it remains relevant, secure, and adaptable to emerging challenges. Today, OAuth serves as the foundation for countless APIs, enabling millions of users to safely and seamlessly connect their applications, devices, and services. As new technologies and use cases continue to emerge, OAuth's journey of evolution and innovation will undoubtedly continue, adapting to meet the needs of a dynamic and interconnected digital world.

Security Best Practices for OAuth 2.0

OAuth 2.0 provides a flexible framework for managing access control and authorization, but its versatility means that developers must carefully implement the protocol to maintain a secure environment. By following established security best practices, organizations can protect sensitive user data, reduce the risk of attacks, and ensure that OAuth 2.0 deployments remain robust and reliable. These practices encompass proper configuration, secure token handling, thorough validation processes, and proactive monitoring, all of which contribute to a stronger and more resilient authorization system.

One of the most fundamental best practices is enforcing HTTPS for all OAuth 2.0 communications. By using HTTPS, sensitive information such as authorization codes, access tokens, and refresh tokens are encrypted in transit, protecting them from interception by attackers. While OAuth 2.0 does not mandate the use of specific cryptographic signatures on each request, it relies on the underlying transport layer for security. Ensuring that HTTPS is properly configured and that certificates are regularly updated and validated is a foundational step in securing any OAuth implementation.

Another critical practice is the use of Proof Key for Code Exchange (PKCE) for public clients. Originally designed for mobile and single-page applications that cannot securely store secrets, PKCE enhances the security of the authorization code flow by introducing a code challenge and code verifier. By requiring the client to prove that it initiated the authorization request, PKCE prevents attackers from intercepting authorization codes and using them to obtain access tokens. Implementing PKCE is considered a best practice even for clients that can store secrets, as it adds an extra layer of protection without introducing significant complexity.

Token management is another important aspect of securing OAuth 2.0. Access tokens should be short-lived to limit the window of opportunity for attackers if a token is compromised. Short token lifespans ensure that even if a token is exposed, it quickly becomes invalid. Additionally, using refresh tokens can improve user experience by enabling clients to obtain new access tokens without requiring the user to reauthenticate. However, refresh tokens themselves must be handled carefully. Storing them securely, rotating them regularly, and ensuring that they are only issued to trusted clients helps reduce the risk of unauthorized access.

Validating tokens is a crucial step in maintaining OAuth security. When a resource server receives a token, it must verify its authenticity before granting access to protected resources. For JSON Web Tokens (JWTs), this means verifying the digital signature and checking claims such as the issuer, audience, and expiration time. For opaque tokens, the resource server should query the authorization server's introspection endpoint to confirm that the token is still active and to retrieve its associated scopes. Thorough token validation ensures that only legitimate, unexpired, and properly scoped tokens are accepted, protecting against unauthorized access and privilege escalation.

Scope management also plays a key role in securing OAuth implementations. By limiting the permissions granted to a client, developers can reduce the potential impact of a compromised token. Scopes should be as narrow as possible, granting access only to the resources and actions that are absolutely necessary. When designing scopes, consider the principle of least privilege. For example, if an application only needs to read user profile information, it should not be granted write access to user data. By enforcing strict scope checks, organizations can prevent clients from performing unintended actions, even if their tokens are valid.

Revocation and monitoring are essential components of a secure OAuth strategy. If a token is suspected to be compromised, it should be revoked immediately. OAuth 2.0 provides a standard revocation endpoint that allows clients and administrators to invalidate tokens. Once revoked, the token can no longer be used to access resources, helping contain potential breaches. Additionally, logging and monitoring all OAuth-related events—including token issuance, validation, and revocation—enables administrators to detect unusual patterns or suspicious behavior. By analyzing these logs and setting up alerts for anomalous activities, organizations can respond quickly to potential security incidents and maintain a secure environment.

Another best practice is to regularly audit and update your OAuth configuration. Over time, new security vulnerabilities may be discovered, and industry standards may evolve. By staying up-to-date with the latest recommendations, such as adopting newer encryption algorithms or implementing additional security headers, developers can ensure that their OAuth 2.0 implementations remain secure against emerging threats. Periodic security assessments, code reviews, and penetration testing can also identify weaknesses and help maintain a strong security posture.

Developer education and proper documentation are also key to a secure OAuth deployment. Ensuring that all team members understand the correct implementation of OAuth flows, the importance of secure token handling, and the consequences of misconfiguration reduces the likelihood of errors. Clear and comprehensive documentation can help developers follow best practices from the start, making it easier to maintain consistent and secure implementations across different teams and projects.

By adhering to these best practices, organizations can significantly improve the security of their OAuth 2.0 deployments. From enforcing HTTPS and using PKCE to managing tokens, validating scopes, and actively monitoring system activity, each step contributes to a more secure and reliable authorization framework. As the digital landscape continues to evolve, maintaining a strong foundation of security best practices ensures that OAuth 2.0 remains an effective and trusted mechanism for managing access to protected resources.

OAuth 2.0 for Mobile Applications

OAuth 2.0 has become the standard for securing access to APIs and user data in mobile applications. As mobile devices play an increasingly central role in our digital lives, developers must ensure that these applications can access resources securely and with minimal friction. By implementing OAuth 2.0 correctly, mobile developers can provide a seamless user experience while safeguarding sensitive data, protecting against unauthorized access, and maintaining trust between the app, the user, and the resource providers.

One of the primary challenges in applying OAuth 2.0 to mobile applications is that these apps are considered public clients. Unlike traditional server-based applications, mobile apps run on end-user devices where secrets, if stored, can be easily extracted. This makes it crucial to design flows and security measures that do not rely on the presence of a secure client secret. Instead, OAuth 2.0 for mobile apps often involves using the authorization code flow combined with Proof Key for Code Exchange (PKCE). PKCE enhances security by adding a dynamically generated code verifier and code challenge, ensuring that only the original app instance that initiated the flow can exchange the authorization code for an access token. By removing the need for a client secret and leveraging PKCE, developers can protect their apps from interception attacks and unauthorized token exchanges.

Mobile platforms also introduce unique considerations around user experience. Unlike a web application that can simply redirect the user's browser to an authorization server's login page, mobile apps must navigate between app screens and external authentication flows without confusing the user. Many developers achieve this by using embedded browser components or in-app browsers, but this approach is generally discouraged due to potential security and usability concerns. Instead, OAuth 2.0 best practices recommend using the device's native browser or a system-level browser tab for authentication. This method ensures that the user's credentials are entered in a trusted environment, isolated from the application itself, reducing the risk of credential theft and maintaining user confidence.

Another important aspect of using OAuth 2.0 in mobile applications is handling tokens securely. Access tokens should never be stored in places that are easily accessible, such as plain-text files, shared preferences on Android, or user defaults on iOS. Instead, developers should use secure storage mechanisms provided by the operating system, such as the iOS Keychain or Android's EncryptedSharedPreferences and Keystore system. Refresh tokens, if used, require even stricter handling because they grant the ability to obtain new access tokens without re-authenticating the user. By carefully managing where and how tokens are stored, developers can limit the risk of tokens being extracted by malicious actors or compromised apps.

The token lifecycle is another critical consideration. Access tokens issued to mobile applications should have short lifespans, ensuring that even if a token is compromised, its usefulness is limited. By issuing short-lived tokens and relying on refresh tokens to maintain session continuity, developers can enhance security without repeatedly prompting the user to log in. This approach balances user convenience with robust security practices, reducing the attack window while maintaining a seamless user experience.

Mobile apps often need to support multiple authentication methods and identity providers, including social logins (such as Google, Facebook, or Apple), enterprise identity providers, and custom backend authentication systems. OAuth 2.0's flexibility makes it well-suited to handle these diverse requirements. For example, an app can integrate with a single OpenID Connect-compatible identity provider or support multiple providers through a common OAuth framework. By standardizing authentication and authorization through OAuth, developers can avoid vendor lock-in and more easily switch identity providers or add new options as the app's needs evolve.

In addition to user authentication, mobile apps may need to perform machine-to-machine authentication for certain tasks, such as syncing data in the background or communicating with backend services that do not involve a user's interaction. In these scenarios, developers can use the client credentials flow or other token-based approaches that do not require the user to be present. By leveraging OAuth 2.0's token infrastructure, mobile apps can securely handle both user-driven and automated operations.

Monitoring and maintaining the security of OAuth 2.0 in mobile applications requires ongoing vigilance. Developers should keep their OAuth library dependencies up to date, apply patches promptly, and regularly review their authentication and token management code for potential vulnerabilities. Additionally, implementing proper logging and monitoring of token exchanges, token usage, and any authentication errors helps developers quickly identify unusual activity or potential attacks. By staying proactive and continuously refining their implementation, developers can ensure that their mobile apps remain secure and trustworthy.

Incorporating OAuth 2.0 into mobile applications offers both security and convenience when done correctly. By following best practices—such as using PKCE, leveraging secure storage, ensuring short token lifespans, and relying on trusted browser environments for authentication—developers can protect user data and provide a reliable experience. As mobile platforms continue to evolve, the flexibility and security features of OAuth 2.0 make it a vital tool for modern app development.

OAuth 2.0 and Microservices Architectures

OAuth 2.0 is a natural fit for securing microservices architectures, where multiple independent services need to communicate securely while maintaining a consistent and manageable authentication model. Microservices emphasize decentralization, scalability, and flexibility, but they also introduce complexities around authorization, token management, and inter-service communication. OAuth 2.0 addresses many of these challenges by providing a standardized framework for issuing, validating, and handling tokens, which can be used to enforce fine-grained access control and ensure that only authorized requests are allowed. By leveraging OAuth 2.0, organizations can secure their microservices architectures without resorting to custom authentication mechanisms that are hard to maintain and scale.

One of the key advantages of using OAuth 2.0 in a microservices environment is the ability to centralize token issuance and validation. Instead of each microservice implementing its own authentication logic, a dedicated authorization server issues tokens that all services can recognize and trust. These tokens carry information—such as the user's identity, roles, and scopes—that each service can use to determine whether a given request is allowed. This centralization simplifies the authentication process and ensures consistent security policies across the entire architecture. With a single source of truth for tokens, organizations can streamline onboarding new services, applying security updates, and auditing access patterns.

In a microservices architecture, it is common for multiple services to interact with each other to fulfill a single client request. For example, a front-end application might call a user profile service, which in turn calls an orders service, which then calls a payment service. Each step in this chain requires authentication and authorization to ensure that only authorized services and clients can access sensitive data or perform critical actions. OAuth 2.0 tokens facilitate this by serving as a portable credential that can be passed from one service to another. Once a client obtains an access token from the authorization server, it can include that token in requests to any microservice that recognizes it. Each service validates the token before processing the request, ensuring that only authorized operations are performed.

OAuth 2.0's scope mechanism is particularly valuable in microservices architectures. Scopes define what actions a client or service is allowed to perform and which resources it can access. By assigning specific scopes to tokens, the authorization server ensures that each service only has the permissions it needs to do its job. For example, a service that handles billing might only receive a token with "read:orders" and "create:invoice" scopes, preventing it from accessing unrelated user profile data. This principle of least privilege helps minimize security risks and limits the potential damage of a compromised token. Furthermore, it enables more granular access control, allowing organizations to adapt their security policies as the architecture evolves and new services are added.

In addition to access tokens, microservices often rely on refresh tokens to maintain long-lived sessions. When a service needs ongoing access to resources, it can use a refresh token to obtain new access tokens without reauthenticating the user. This approach reduces the number of times a client needs to prompt the user for credentials, improving the overall user experience. However, in a microservices environment, it's essential to handle refresh tokens carefully. Secure storage, short-lived access tokens, and regular token rotation help prevent misuse and limit the impact of compromised credentials.

Another important consideration in microservices architectures is token validation. Each microservice must verify that the token it receives is valid and has not expired. In many implementations, this involves checking the token's signature (for JSON Web Tokens, or

JWTs) or calling the authorization server's introspection endpoint. By validating tokens at each step, services ensure that they only process authorized requests. This decentralized validation allows services to operate independently while maintaining a consistent level of security. Additionally, token validation ensures that revoked tokens or tokens with insufficient scopes are promptly rejected, preventing unauthorized access even in complex service-to-service communication scenarios.

OAuth 2.0 also helps address compliance and auditing requirements in microservices environments. By using a centralized authorization server to issue and manage tokens, organizations can maintain detailed logs of token usage, including which services requested tokens, which scopes were granted, and when tokens were revoked or refreshed. These logs provide valuable insights for auditing access patterns, detecting anomalies, and demonstrating compliance with industry regulations. The ability to trace every request back to an issued token and the associated user or client helps organizations maintain a strong security posture and meet regulatory obligations.

As microservices architectures grow and evolve, OAuth 2.0's extensibility becomes increasingly important. Organizations can integrate additional security features, such as Proof Key for Code Exchange (PKCE) for public clients, token revocation endpoints for real-time access control, and token exchange mechanisms for handling complex service-to-service interactions. By building on the OAuth 2.0 framework, developers can adapt their security models to meet new challenges without overhauling their entire authentication infrastructure. This flexibility ensures that microservices architectures remain secure, scalable, and responsive to changing requirements.

OAuth 2.0's ability to provide standardized token-based authorization, enforce fine-grained access control, and centralize token management makes it an ideal choice for securing microservices architectures. By leveraging these capabilities, organizations can simplify their security models, reduce the complexity of managing credentials across multiple services, and ensure that each request is authenticated and authorized according to consistent, well-defined policies. This approach not only enhances security but also improves the maintainability and scalability of the overall architecture.

Understanding the OIDC Discovery Document

The OpenID Connect (OIDC) Discovery Document is a critical component of the OIDC protocol, designed to simplify and standardize the way client applications interact with identity providers. At its core, the Discovery Document provides a single, well-defined endpoint where all the necessary metadata about an OpenID provider (OP) can be retrieved. By consolidating information such as endpoint URLs, supported signing algorithms, token formats, and available scopes, the Discovery Document enables dynamic and automated configuration of clients, reducing manual configuration errors and enhancing interoperability across various implementations.

The Discovery Document itself is a JSON file that lives at a standardized location within the OpenID provider's domain. The URL is typically structured as .well-known/openid-configuration, making it easy for client applications to locate. For example, if the OpenID provider's base URL is https://example.com, the Discovery Document would be available at https://example.com/.well-known/openid-configuration. By following this convention, clients can automatically discover the provider's capabilities without needing hard-coded values, making integrations more robust and easier to maintain over time.

One of the key elements of the Discovery Document is the list of endpoint URLs that clients need to interact with. These endpoints include the authorization endpoint, token endpoint, userinfo endpoint, and revocation endpoint, among others. Each of these endpoints serves a specific purpose within the OIDC flow. For instance, the authorization endpoint is where users authenticate and grant consent, while the token endpoint is where clients exchange authorization codes for tokens. By centralizing these URLs in the Discovery Document, OIDC ensures that clients always have access to the correct locations, even if the provider's endpoints change. This dynamic discovery process reduces the need for manual updates and minimizes the risk of configuration errors.

In addition to endpoint URLs, the Discovery Document includes information about the provider's supported features and capabilities.

For example, it lists the supported response types, grant types, and token signing algorithms. This allows clients to determine the best approach for interacting with the provider. If a provider supports RS256 for token signatures, the client can prepare to verify those tokens using the corresponding public keys. Similarly, if the provider supports the authorization code flow, the client knows it can obtain an authorization code and exchange it for tokens. This metadata ensures that clients can tailor their behavior to the provider's capabilities, improving compatibility and reducing the likelihood of integration issues.

The Discovery Document also defines the location of the provider's JSON Web Key Set (JWKS). The JWKS is a JSON document that contains the public keys used by the provider to sign tokens. By referencing the JWKS URL in the Discovery Document, clients can dynamically retrieve the keys they need to validate ID tokens and other JWTs. This eliminates the need to manually distribute and update public keys, making the process more secure and manageable. When the provider rotates keys or updates its signing algorithms, clients automatically pick up the changes by fetching the updated JWKS, ensuring continuous token validation without interruption.

Scopes and claims supported by the provider are another critical piece of metadata found in the Discovery Document. Scopes define the level of access that the client can request, such as reading a user's profile information or accessing their email address. Claims, on the other hand, represent the specific attributes returned in the ID token or userinfo response. By including this information in the Discovery Document, providers give clients a clear understanding of what data is available and how to request it. This transparency helps clients construct requests that align with the provider's policies and ensures that they receive the appropriate information in return.

The Discovery Document also includes important security-related parameters, such as supported authentication methods for the token endpoint. Some providers may require clients to authenticate using a client secret, while others might support private key JWTs or mutual TLS. By listing the supported authentication methods, the Discovery Document helps clients choose the appropriate approach for securing their token requests. This information is crucial for maintaining a secure interaction between the client and the provider, as it ensures that tokens are obtained only through authorized, authenticated channels.

By consolidating all of this metadata in one place, the OIDC Discovery Document greatly simplifies the process of integrating with an OpenID provider. Instead of relying on hard-coded values and manual configuration, clients can programmatically fetch the Discovery Document and adjust their behavior accordingly. This dynamic configuration capability is especially valuable in large-scale environments, where multiple providers, regions, or environments might be in use. With the Discovery Document, updates to endpoints, algorithms, or supported features are handled seamlessly, without requiring code changes or manual intervention.

In practice, the Discovery Document is often the first point of contact when a client begins interacting with an OpenID provider. By querying the well-known URL, the client retrieves a comprehensive map of the provider's capabilities, which it can then use to guide its authentication and token handling processes. This approach not only reduces the complexity of initial setup but also ensures that integrations remain stable and up-to-date as the provider's configuration evolves over time. The Discovery Document's standardized format, consistent location, and comprehensive metadata make it a cornerstone of the OpenID Connect ecosystem, enabling smoother integrations, better security, and greater interoperability across a wide range of applications and services.

Client Registration and Dynamic Client Registration

In OAuth 2.0 and OpenID Connect, client registration is the process by which an application, referred to as a client, is introduced to the authorization server so that it can request tokens and access protected resources. By registering a client, the authorization server knows what permissions the client is requesting, what redirection endpoints it uses, and how it authenticates. This step is essential for establishing trust between the client application and the authorization server, as well as for ensuring secure and controlled interactions. Traditionally, client registration has been a manual process, but dynamic client registration streamlines this by allowing clients to register themselves programmatically, reducing administrative overhead and increasing flexibility.

At the heart of client registration is the concept of a client ID. The client ID is a unique identifier issued by the authorization server to each registered application. It serves as a public identifier, allowing the authorization server to recognize the application when it makes requests. Alongside the client ID, a confidential client is typically assigned a client secret, a private key-like credential that the client uses to authenticate itself to the authorization server. This client secret must be handled carefully, as it proves the identity of the client and is required when the client requests tokens. For public clients—such as single-page applications or mobile apps—client secrets are not used, as these applications cannot securely store secrets. Instead, other mechanisms like Proof Key for Code Exchange (PKCE) are employed to ensure secure interactions.

During the registration process, the client provides the authorization server with a set of metadata. This metadata includes redirect URIs, which tell the authorization server where to send users after they authenticate. It also specifies the client's intended grant types, such as authorization code or implicit, and the scopes it wishes to request. Some clients may also provide additional details, such as a logo, a policy URL, or a set of requested claims. By collecting this information upfront, the authorization server can enforce security policies, ensure that the client is using authorized endpoints, and present users with accurate information when they are prompted to grant access.

The traditional manual registration process typically involves a developer contacting the administrator of the authorization server, submitting the necessary metadata, and receiving a client ID and secret. While this approach works well in environments with a small number of clients or when high levels of manual oversight are required, it becomes cumbersome and error-prone as the number of applications grows. Each new client requires administrative intervention, and any changes to the client's configuration must go through the same manual process. This can create bottlenecks, slow down development, and increase the risk of misconfiguration or inconsistent metadata.

Dynamic client registration, as defined by the OAuth 2.0 Dynamic Client Registration specification, addresses these challenges by allowing clients to self-register with the authorization server. Instead of relying on an administrator to manually input metadata, the client sends a registration request directly to the authorization server's registration endpoint. This request includes all the necessary information, such as redirect URIs, grant types, and requested scopes. The authorization server processes the request, validates the provided data, and returns a response that includes the client ID, and potentially a client secret if the client is confidential. This automated process reduces administrative overhead, speeds up onboarding for new applications, and ensures that clients are registered consistently and accurately.

Dynamic client registration also enables more flexible and scalable application development workflows. In environments where applications are frequently deployed, updated, or retired—such as microservices architectures or continuous delivery pipelines— dynamic registration allows new instances of applications to register themselves without manual intervention. This ensures that as the environment evolves, the authorization server always has an up-to-date list of registered clients, and the clients themselves can quickly adapt to changes. By eliminating the need for manual coordination, dynamic registration supports faster iteration, more reliable configurations, and a streamlined approach to managing large numbers of clients.

Another benefit of dynamic client registration is the ability to handle different trust levels and access policies for various types of clients. For example, an authorization server can require that certain sensitive scopes or grants be pre-approved or restricted to certain trusted clients. Other clients might be allowed to register dynamically but limited to requesting specific, lower-privilege scopes. This granularity enables a more nuanced security model, allowing the authorization server to maintain strict controls while still supporting a broad range of applications.

Security is a critical consideration in both manual and dynamic client registration. When clients register, the authorization server must validate the provided metadata to ensure it is well-formed, matches expected patterns, and does not include malicious or unexpected values. For example, redirect URIs should be carefully vetted to prevent open redirects or other attacks. Additionally, any secrets generated during registration should be transmitted securely and stored safely. In dynamic registration scenarios, the authorization server may also authenticate the client or require certain prerequisites before allowing registration. These measures help ensure that only legitimate applications can register and that the resulting configuration is both secure and trustworthy.

The evolution from manual client registration to dynamic client registration represents a significant step forward in making OAuth 2.0 and OpenID Connect more scalable, efficient, and developer-friendly. By allowing clients to register themselves programmatically, dynamic registration reduces the overhead of managing large application ecosystems, supports agile development practices, and ensures that registration data remains consistent and up-to-date. Whether implemented through traditional means or dynamically, client registration is a foundational process that ensures the security, reliability, and flexibility of OAuth-based authorization systems.

Token Exchange and Chaining

Token exchange and chaining are advanced techniques in OAuth 2.0 that allow clients and services to transform, delegate, or adapt tokens as they move through various components of a distributed architecture. As organizations build increasingly complex ecosystems of microservices, APIs, and third-party integrations, the need for controlled and seamless token management grows. Token exchange enables one token, originally issued for a particular use case, to be exchanged for another token with different attributes or permissions. Token chaining involves passing tokens through multiple layers of services, ensuring that each service in the chain only receives the minimum level of access it requires. Together, these approaches help maintain secure, flexible, and efficient token flows in modern OAuth-based environments.

The OAuth 2.0 Token Exchange specification defines a standardized framework for exchanging tokens. This process typically begins with a client or service holding a token that was issued by an authorization server. The client then requests a new token from the same or another authorization server, specifying the intended audience and scope of the new token. The original token acts as proof of the client's identity or authorization, allowing the authorization server to issue a token that is better suited to the requested operation. For example, a mobile application might use a user's access token to obtain a service token that grants limited access to a backend API. By leveraging token exchange, organizations can ensure that each component of their architecture operates with precisely the permissions it needs, without exposing broader-scoped tokens beyond their intended context.

One common scenario for token exchange is in multi-service architectures where a single request traverses multiple backend systems. A frontend application might start by obtaining a user's access token, which grants broad permissions. As this token passes through various backend services, each service can exchange it for a more restrictive token tailored to the specific task at hand. For instance, a data-processing service might exchange the original token for one that only allows read-only access to a data store, while a billing service might exchange it for a token that permits updating payment records. By exchanging tokens at each step, the architecture enforces the principle of least privilege, ensuring that no service holds more permissions than it needs at any given time.

Another benefit of token exchange is the ability to delegate access. Delegation involves issuing a token that allows a third party or another service to act on behalf of the original token holder. For example, a scheduling service might exchange a user's access token for a token that lets a notification service send reminders on the user's behalf. The exchanged token has a specific audience and scope, ensuring that the notification service cannot access other resources or perform actions beyond its intended role. This approach maintains a clear separation of responsibilities, reduces the risk of over-permissioned tokens, and enables secure, controlled delegation of tasks within complex workflows.

Token chaining complements token exchange by ensuring that tokens passed between services remain tightly controlled and contextually appropriate. In a chained token scenario, the original token might include a limited set of claims or scopes, and each subsequent service in the chain can add or restrict claims as needed. For instance, a frontend application might receive a token with user-level scopes, and as it calls downstream services, each service validates and augments the token with additional information relevant to its function. This dynamic adjustment of token attributes ensures that the token remains valid, relevant, and secure throughout its lifecycle.

Both token exchange and chaining rely on strong validation and secure token handling practices. When a token is presented for exchange, the authorization server must verify its authenticity, ensure it has not expired, and confirm that the requesting party is authorized to perform the exchange. Similarly, each service in a token chain must validate incoming tokens, ensuring that they come from a trusted source, have the appropriate claims, and meet the required security policies. By enforcing these checks at each step, organizations maintain the integrity of their token flows and prevent unauthorized access or token misuse.

One challenge in implementing token exchange and chaining is managing the complexity of multiple token types, audiences, and scopes. As tokens are exchanged and passed between services, developers must carefully define and document the relationships between different token types and ensure that all components of the system are aware of the token hierarchy. Establishing clear guidelines for token issuance, exchange, and chaining helps prevent confusion, reduces the likelihood of misconfiguration, and ensures that the system operates smoothly under a unified set of security policies.

Token exchange and chaining also support compliance and auditing efforts. By ensuring that each token is issued for a specific purpose and is valid only within its intended context, organizations can demonstrate a higher level of control over their authorization flows. Detailed logs of token exchanges and chained token usage provide valuable insights into who accessed what, when, and under what conditions. This transparency not only strengthens security but also helps meet regulatory requirements and supports incident investigation.

As modern systems become more distributed and interdependent, token exchange and chaining offer powerful tools for managing access in a secure, scalable, and flexible way. By adapting tokens to fit specific contexts and ensuring that each service operates within the boundaries of its assigned permissions, these techniques help maintain a robust and well-structured authorization framework.

The Role of JSON Web Tokens (JWT)

JSON Web Tokens (JWTs) have emerged as a critical building block in modern authentication and authorization systems. Designed as a lightweight and self-contained format, JWTs enable secure and efficient communication of claims—statements about a subject—between parties. In the context of OAuth 2.0 and OpenID Connect, JWTs serve multiple roles, from carrying user identity information in ID tokens to granting access to APIs via access tokens. By understanding the structure, functionality, and best practices associated with JWTs, developers can harness their full potential while ensuring robust security.

A JWT is a compact, URL-safe string composed of three parts: the header, the payload, and the signature. The header typically specifies the type of token—JWT—and the algorithm used to sign it, such as RS256 or HS256. The payload contains the claims, which can include standard fields like sub (subject identifier), iss (issuer), exp (expiration time), and custom fields that convey additional information. Finally, the signature is generated using the specified algorithm and a secret or private key, ensuring that the token's contents cannot be tampered with. When a recipient receives a JWT, they can verify the signature using the corresponding public key or shared secret, confirming that the token is authentic and has not been altered.

One of the primary advantages of JWTs is their self-contained nature. Unlike opaque tokens, which require the recipient to query a database or an introspection endpoint to retrieve associated information, JWTs carry all necessary claims within the token itself. This allows services to validate tokens locally, without additional network calls, leading to reduced latency and improved performance. For example, an API that receives a JWT as an access token can decode it, verify its signature, and immediately determine whether the request is authorized, without having to contact an external authorization server.

JWTs also play a central role in OpenID Connect, where they are used as ID tokens to convey identity information about the authenticated user. The ID token, a specific type of JWT, includes claims about the user, such as their unique identifier (sub), the issuer (iss), the audience (aud), and when the token was issued (iat). By verifying the ID token's signature and checking these claims, the relying party (RP)—the application receiving the token—can confidently identify the user and grant access to appropriate resources. This streamlined approach makes JWTs a cornerstone of the OpenID Connect protocol, enabling secure single sign-on (SSO) and identity federation.

In OAuth 2.0, JWTs are often used as access tokens. When issued as access tokens, JWTs include claims that help APIs determine the token's validity and the client's permissions. Common claims might include the token's expiration time (exp), the scopes granted (scope), and the client ID (client_id). By examining these claims, the resource server can enforce fine-grained access control and ensure that only authorized clients can access protected endpoints. Since the token is signed, the resource server can trust that the information it contains has not been altered by a malicious party.

Another important role of JWTs is enabling token validation across distributed systems. In a microservices architecture, where multiple services need to verify tokens independently, the self-contained nature of JWTs is especially valuable. Each service can independently verify the JWT's signature using a shared public key, without relying on a centralized token store or making introspection requests. This reduces complexity and improves scalability, as each service can operate autonomously while still maintaining a consistent and secure authorization framework.

JWTs are also used to implement custom claims that carry application-specific information. For instance, a company's internal API might include a custom claim that indicates the user's department or their access level within the organization. These custom claims allow developers to tailor the token's contents to the application's unique requirements, making JWTs a versatile tool for implementing complex authorization logic. By defining and standardizing the use of these claims, organizations can ensure that their services interpret tokens consistently, reducing the likelihood of misconfiguration or security gaps.

Despite their many benefits, JWTs must be handled carefully to maintain security. Developers should always use strong signing algorithms and secure key management practices. It's essential to regularly rotate signing keys, implement appropriate token lifetimes, and revoke tokens when necessary. When designing a system that relies on JWTs, it's important to verify not only the signature but also the claims, including checking the iss (issuer) and aud (audience) fields, and ensuring that the token has not expired. By following these best practices, developers can leverage JWTs' strengths while minimizing potential risks.

JSON Web Tokens play a foundational role in modern authentication and authorization. By providing a self-contained, verifiable, and extensible token format, JWTs enable secure communication of claims, improve performance by allowing local validation, and enhance flexibility in handling user identity and permissions. As a result, JWTs have become an essential component of OAuth 2.0, OpenID Connect, and numerous other protocols and frameworks, helping developers build secure and scalable systems for today's distributed and interconnected world.

OAuth 2.0 in Single-Page Applications (SPAs)

Single-page applications (SPAs) have become a popular choice for delivering dynamic, user-friendly web experiences. Unlike traditional web applications that reload entire pages upon user interactions, SPAs rely heavily on JavaScript to dynamically update content without requiring a full page refresh. While this approach provides a smoother and more responsive experience, it also introduces unique challenges for implementing secure authentication and authorization. OAuth 2.0, when applied correctly, can address these challenges and provide a secure framework for SPAs to obtain access tokens, authenticate users, and protect sensitive resources.

One of the key challenges in using OAuth 2.0 with SPAs is that these applications are considered public clients. Public clients are inherently less secure than confidential clients because they cannot securely store secrets. Since the entire codebase of an SPA runs in the user's browser, any secret included in the application's code is potentially exposed to anyone who inspects the code. As a result, SPAs cannot rely on traditional client secrets to prove their identity to an authorization server. Instead, OAuth 2.0 provides alternative mechanisms—such as the authorization code flow with Proof Key for Code Exchange (PKCE)—to secure SPAs without requiring client secrets.

The authorization code flow with PKCE is widely recognized as the best practice for SPAs. In this flow, the SPA generates a random code verifier and a code challenge at the start of the authentication process. The code challenge, derived from the code verifier using a hashing function, is sent to the authorization server along with the authorization request. When the user authenticates and grants consent, the authorization server returns an authorization code. The SPA then exchanges this code for an access token, sending the original code verifier as proof that it initiated the request. The authorization server verifies that the code challenge and code verifier match before issuing the token. By using PKCE, the authorization code flow ensures that even if the authorization code is intercepted, it cannot be used to obtain a token without the code verifier.

Another consideration for SPAs is where and how to store tokens securely. Since SPAs run entirely in the browser, tokens are often stored in memory or in the browser's local storage. However, using local storage or session storage carries certain risks. Tokens stored in these locations can be accessed by malicious scripts if the application is vulnerable to cross-site scripting (XSS) attacks. To mitigate these risks, developers should prioritize securing the application against XSS and consider using in-memory storage as a safer alternative. Storing tokens in memory ensures that they are not persisted beyond the current session and reduces the attack surface. While this approach means tokens will be lost if the user refreshes the page, the trade-off in improved security is often worthwhile.

Token lifecycle management is another critical aspect of using OAuth 2.0 in SPAs. Access tokens issued to SPAs are typically short-lived to minimize the impact of token theft. Once an access token expires, the SPA must obtain a new one to maintain a seamless user experience. This is often done by using refresh tokens, which can be securely stored in a secure cookie or accessed through a secure server-side endpoint. However, refresh tokens must be handled carefully. For SPAs that cannot securely store refresh tokens, developers may rely on silent reauthentication techniques. For example, the SPA can redirect the user to the authorization server's authorization endpoint behind the scenes, allowing the user to remain logged in without seeing a login prompt. This approach keeps the user experience smooth while ensuring that tokens remain current and secure.

Another important consideration is the use of CORS (Cross-Origin Resource Sharing) and secure headers. SPAs frequently make API calls to domains different from the one serving the application. Properly configured CORS headers on the API side ensure that only authorized origins can access protected resources. Additionally, implementing Content Security Policy (CSP) headers helps protect against XSS attacks by restricting the sources from which scripts can be loaded. By securing both the API endpoints and the SPA's environment, developers can prevent unauthorized access and reduce the risk of token theft or misuse.

In addition to these technical measures, transparency and user trust play a significant role in using OAuth 2.0 with SPAs. Users should always understand which permissions the application is requesting and why. The consent screen presented during the authorization process should clearly state the scopes being requested and the intended use of the data. By providing this clarity, SPAs can build user confidence, ensuring that individuals are comfortable granting access to their resources.

OAuth 2.0, when applied with best practices, enables SPAs to authenticate users, obtain tokens securely, and interact with protected APIs without relying on insecure workarounds. By leveraging the authorization code flow with PKCE, focusing on secure token storage, implementing proper token lifecycle management, and adhering to strong security headers, developers can maintain a high level of security while delivering the responsive, user-friendly experience that SPAs are known for.

Common OAuth 2.0 Pitfalls and How to Avoid Them

Implementing OAuth 2.0 can greatly enhance the security and flexibility of your authentication and authorization processes. However, many developers encounter common pitfalls that can undermine the integrity of their implementations. These issues often stem from misconfigurations, improper token handling, or an incomplete understanding of the OAuth 2.0 specification. By identifying these challenges and taking proactive steps to avoid them, you can ensure that your OAuth 2.0 deployment is both secure and robust.

One of the most frequent mistakes is relying on implicit flows or outdated practices that are no longer recommended. Historically, the implicit flow was used in certain scenarios to simplify authentication, especially for single-page applications. However, it has since been deemed less secure due to the exposure of access tokens in the browser's URL fragment and its vulnerability to token interception. Instead, modern best practices advocate for the authorization code flow with Proof Key for Code Exchange (PKCE). PKCE enhances security by requiring a code verifier and code challenge, making it significantly harder for attackers to misuse authorization codes or tokens. By adopting PKCE and avoiding implicit flows, you can reduce the risk of token theft and improve the overall security of your implementation.

Another common issue is inadequate token validation on the resource server. Many developers mistakenly assume that if a token is issued by a trusted authorization server, it can always be trusted at face value. In reality, each time a resource server receives a token, it should verify key claims such as the token's issuer (iss), audience (aud), and expiration (exp). Additionally, if the token is a JSON Web Token (JWT), the resource server must validate its signature using the appropriate public key. Failing to perform these checks can allow attackers to reuse stolen or manipulated tokens, granting unauthorized access to protected resources. By ensuring proper token validation at every step, you can prevent unauthorized access and maintain the integrity of your API.

Improper handling of refresh tokens is another frequent pitfall. Refresh tokens are intended to allow clients to obtain new access tokens without requiring the user to reauthenticate. However, if not stored securely, refresh tokens can become a target for attackers. Storing refresh tokens in insecure locations, such as local storage in a browser or plaintext on a client device, increases the risk of compromise. Once an attacker gains access to a refresh token, they can generate new access tokens and continue accessing resources even after the original access token has expired. To avoid this, always store refresh tokens in secure environments, such as encrypted storage mechanisms or secure server-side storage, and implement proper token rotation and revocation policies.

Misuse of overly broad scopes can also lead to unintended consequences. When requesting access tokens, clients should only request the minimum scopes needed for their functionality. Requesting unnecessary scopes or granting tokens with excessive privileges increases the potential damage if a token is compromised. For instance, a token with both read and write access to user data may not be necessary if the client only needs to read data. By adopting the principle of least privilege and carefully defining scopes, you can limit the impact of token compromise and ensure that clients have only the access they truly need.

Another common mistake is neglecting to implement robust token expiration policies. Tokens with long lifetimes provide attackers with a larger window of opportunity if they manage to steal the token. While long-lived tokens might seem convenient, they significantly increase risk. Instead, access tokens should have short lifespans, and clients should rely on refresh tokens to maintain access. Short-lived tokens ensure that even if a token is stolen, it quickly becomes invalid. By enforcing strict expiration times and using refresh tokens responsibly, you can improve security while maintaining a seamless user experience.

Developers also frequently underestimate the importance of monitoring and logging. Without proper logging, it can be difficult to detect and respond to suspicious activity or potential breaches. OAuth 2.0 implementations should log key events, such as token issuance, token validation failures, token revocations, and token refresh attempts. Monitoring these logs enables early detection of unusual patterns, such as repeated failed token exchanges or unexpected token usage from unfamiliar IP addresses. Implementing alerts and periodic reviews of these logs allows organizations to respond quickly to potential threats and maintain a secure environment.

Finally, a lack of clear documentation and well-defined processes can lead to implementation errors. Developers may make incorrect assumptions about how the authorization server or resource server operates, leading to misconfigurations or unintended security gaps. Ensuring that all team members understand the OAuth 2.0 flows, the role of each component, and the security requirements is crucial. Providing clear, comprehensive documentation—along with internal training or code reviews—helps maintain consistent and correct implementations across different teams and projects.

By recognizing these common pitfalls and adopting best practices, developers can build secure, reliable OAuth 2.0 implementations. Using modern flows like PKCE, performing thorough token validation, handling tokens securely, enforcing strict scope and expiration policies, maintaining proper logging, and fostering a well-documented and well-trained development process all contribute to a stronger, more resilient authorization system.

Debugging OAuth 2.0 Implementations

Debugging OAuth 2.0 implementations can be a complex and challenging task due to the number of moving parts involved. From understanding the flows and examining HTTP responses to troubleshooting token-related issues, developers often find themselves navigating through multiple layers of potential problems. Despite these challenges, a systematic approach can help identify and resolve issues more efficiently. By focusing on key aspects such as endpoint configurations, request parameters, response codes, token handling, and logging, you can pinpoint the root causes of errors and ensure a more reliable OAuth integration.

One of the first steps in debugging OAuth 2.0 issues is to carefully review the configuration of your authorization server and client application. Often, misconfigurations in client IDs, client secrets, redirect URIs, or scope definitions lead to authentication failures or unexpected errors. For example, a mismatch between the registered redirect URI in the authorization server and the URI included in the client's request will typically result in an invalid request error. Checking these configurations for typos, incorrect values, or inconsistent environment settings is crucial. Ensuring that each parameter is correctly set according to the provider's documentation can prevent many common pitfalls and reduce the time spent troubleshooting.

Another critical area to investigate is the HTTP requests and responses involved in the OAuth flow. Tools like browser developer consoles, network inspectors, or API monitoring tools can help you capture and analyze the raw HTTP traffic. By inspecting the authorization request sent to the authorization server's endpoint, you can verify that all required parameters—such as client_id, response_type, scope, and redirect_uri—are included and correctly formatted. On the response side, examining the status codes and error messages returned by the authorization server can provide valuable clues. Common error responses, such as invalid_request, invalid_client, or invalid_grant, often include an error_description field that gives more detail about what went wrong. Paying attention to these error messages and response codes is essential for identifying where the process is failing.

Token-related issues are another frequent source of debugging headaches. Access tokens, refresh tokens, and ID tokens must all be properly issued, handled, and validated. If you encounter token validation errors, it's important to verify that the tokens are being decoded and verified correctly. For JSON Web Tokens (JWTs), this means checking the signature using the authorization server's public key and validating claims such as the issuer (iss), audience (aud), expiration (exp), and not-before (nbf) timestamps. If any of these checks fail, the token may be rejected by the resource server. Ensuring that your token validation logic aligns with the provider's specifications can eliminate a significant source of errors.

Refresh token issues often arise when clients attempt to use an expired, revoked, or improperly scoped refresh token. In these cases, reviewing the token's lifecycle is crucial. For example, if a refresh token is used after it has expired, the token endpoint will return an error, preventing the client from obtaining a new access token. Logging and monitoring the issuance, storage, and usage of refresh tokens can help pinpoint where things go wrong. If refresh tokens are revoked due to user actions or security policies, the client must gracefully handle the resulting errors and prompt the user for reauthentication when necessary.

Logging and monitoring play a critical role in debugging OAuth 2.0 implementations. By enabling detailed logging on both the client and server sides, you can capture information about each step of the authorization process. Logs can show you when a request was received, what parameters were included, whether tokens were successfully issued, and how the server responded to each step. When an error occurs, well-structured logs can immediately point you to the underlying cause—be it a missing parameter, an invalid token, or a misconfigured endpoint. In addition to local logging, integrating application performance monitoring (APM) tools or centralized logging platforms can provide a broader view of OAuth-related activity, helping you identify patterns, recurring issues, and potential optimizations.

Understanding the nuances of different OAuth flows and grant types is also key to effective debugging. Each grant type—authorization code, implicit, client credentials, and resource owner password credentials—has its own set of parameters, expectations, and potential pitfalls. For example, the authorization code flow with Proof Key for Code Exchange (PKCE) introduces a code challenge and code verifier that must match. If these values are not correctly generated, stored, and sent, the token exchange will fail. Similarly, in the client credentials flow, ensuring that the client ID and client secret are valid and properly authenticated is critical. Familiarizing yourself with the expected inputs and outputs for each flow type allows you to more quickly identify where the process breaks down.

Lastly, don't underestimate the value of testing against known-good configurations or reference implementations. If you're consistently encountering issues, try using a test environment or a standard OAuth provider to verify that your client's implementation works as intended. Once you confirm that the client behaves correctly with a known provider, you can narrow down the source of the problem to your specific authorization server configuration or environment. Comparing successful and unsuccessful flows can highlight discrepancies, helping you isolate and fix the root cause of the issue.

Debugging OAuth 2.0 implementations requires a methodical approach that combines careful configuration review, thorough request and response analysis, proper token handling, comprehensive logging, and a solid understanding of OAuth flows. By following these steps, you can quickly identify and address common issues, leading to a more reliable and secure authentication and authorization setup.

Securing Confidential Clients

In the OAuth 2.0 framework, a confidential client is an application that can securely store credentials—such as client secrets—and is typically hosted on a server that users cannot directly access. Because these applications can maintain and protect private information, they are considered more secure than public clients, which run in environments where secrets cannot be safely kept, such as browsers or mobile devices. However, simply having the ability to store secrets doesn't automatically make an implementation secure. Developers and administrators must take deliberate steps to ensure that confidential clients are properly secured and protected against both external and internal threats.

One of the fundamental aspects of securing a confidential client is the correct handling and storage of the client secret. The client secret is essentially the private key that the client uses to authenticate with the authorization server. If this secret is exposed, attackers could impersonate the client, request tokens, and gain unauthorized access to protected resources. To prevent such breaches, confidential clients should store secrets in encrypted environments. For instance, secrets can be kept in hardware security modules (HSMs), dedicated secure key stores, or encrypted configuration files that are only accessible to trusted application processes. Using robust encryption algorithms and ensuring that the encryption keys themselves are stored securely is vital. Regularly rotating client secrets further reduces risk by limiting the exposure of any single secret over time.

Another key practice is implementing strict access controls. Even within a controlled server environment, not all users or processes should have access to the client secret. Role-based access control (RBAC) or attribute-based access control (ABAC) policies can ensure that only the necessary components or personnel can retrieve or modify the secret. Developers should design the application so that the secret is only accessible at runtime by the code paths that need it. For example, a web application that uses OAuth 2.0 for user authentication may only require the secret when exchanging an authorization code for a token. By isolating these code paths and limiting the scope of secret usage, you reduce the likelihood of accidental or malicious exposure.

Network security is another important layer in securing confidential clients. All communications between the confidential client and the authorization server must occur over secure channels using HTTPS. Transport Layer Security (TLS) ensures that the data transmitted—including the client secret, tokens, and other sensitive information—cannot be intercepted by attackers. Additionally, using mutual TLS (mTLS) for client authentication can strengthen security by requiring both the client and the authorization server to present certificates. This helps verify that the client is legitimate and adds an extra layer of protection beyond the client secret. Implementing certificate pinning and ensuring that certificates are regularly updated and properly managed further enhances the security of these communications.

Developers must also consider the principle of least privilege. Confidential clients often request certain scopes or permissions when obtaining tokens. By carefully reviewing and limiting the scopes requested, the client minimizes the damage that could be done if a token is compromised. For example, if the client only needs to read user profile information, it should not request write access to user data. Similarly, if the client only needs access to a single API, it should not request global permissions. By narrowly defining the scopes and permissions required, you reduce the potential impact of a breach and ensure that the client operates with the minimum level of access necessary.

Another best practice is to monitor and log all interactions involving the confidential client's credentials. By maintaining comprehensive logs, administrators can track when the client secret is used, who accessed it, and under what circumstances. These logs can be integrated into a centralized logging system or a security information and event management (SIEM) platform to provide real-time alerts if unusual activity is detected. For instance, if the secret is accessed outside of normal operational hours or from unexpected IP addresses, automated alerts can help security teams respond quickly. Logging also supports auditing and compliance efforts, ensuring that the organization can demonstrate proper handling and protection of sensitive credentials.

Regular security assessments and vulnerability scans should be conducted on the systems hosting confidential clients. By identifying and remediating potential vulnerabilities—such as unpatched software, outdated libraries, or misconfigured network settings—organizations can prevent many common attacks. Penetration testing, code reviews, and continuous security scans help ensure that the environment remains secure over time. Additionally, staying up-to-date with the latest security advisories and implementing recommended patches promptly reduces the risk of exploitation.

Finally, confidential clients should be designed with an incident response plan in mind. If a client secret is ever suspected to be compromised, the organization must be able to quickly rotate the secret, revoke any tokens issued with the old secret, and update the application's configuration. Having a well-defined process for secret rotation, combined with tools that support seamless updates, ensures that security incidents can be addressed rapidly and effectively, minimizing downtime and exposure.

Securing confidential clients requires a multi-layered approach that goes beyond simply storing a client secret. By implementing robust encryption, enforcing strict access controls, using secure communication channels, adhering to the principle of least privilege, maintaining thorough logging, conducting regular security assessments, and preparing for secret rotation, organizations can ensure that their confidential clients remain secure and reliable. These best practices help protect sensitive credentials, prevent unauthorized access, and maintain the integrity of the OAuth 2.0 ecosystem.

Public Clients and Security Challenges

Public clients present unique security challenges in OAuth 2.0 implementations. Unlike confidential clients, which can securely store secrets and run on protected servers, public clients operate in environments where they cannot safeguard credentials or other sensitive information. Mobile applications, single-page applications (SPAs), and desktop apps all fall into the category of public clients. Since they cannot rely on client secrets to authenticate with authorization servers, developers must adopt other measures to secure tokens, protect user data, and mitigate risks.

One of the primary security concerns for public clients is that their code and storage are exposed to end users and potential attackers. In mobile apps, for example, anyone can decompile the app's code or examine the resources stored on a device. Similarly, in SPAs, all JavaScript code runs in the user's browser, making it accessible to anyone who views the page's source. This exposure means that if a client secret were embedded in the code, it would be trivially easy for an attacker to extract it. As a result, public clients are typically not issued client secrets, and the security model must rely on other mechanisms to prevent unauthorized access.

One such mechanism is the use of Proof Key for Code Exchange (PKCE). PKCE was introduced to secure the authorization code flow in environments where client secrets cannot be used. Instead of requiring a client secret, PKCE uses a dynamically generated code verifier and a code challenge. The client generates a random code verifier and then creates a code challenge—typically a hashed version of the verifier—before initiating the authorization request. When the authorization server issues the authorization code, the client must include the original code verifier when exchanging the code for a token. The authorization server verifies that the code challenge and verifier match before granting a token. This approach ensures that even if an attacker intercepts the authorization code, they cannot exchange it for a token without the corresponding verifier, which they do not possess. By using PKCE, public clients can significantly improve their security posture without relying on client secrets.

Another challenge for public clients is securely storing access tokens and refresh tokens. Since public clients run in environments where storage is not inherently secure, the risk of token theft is higher. In mobile apps, storing tokens in plaintext or using insecure storage mechanisms increases the likelihood that an attacker can extract them. In SPAs, storing tokens in browser local storage or session storage exposes them to malicious scripts injected through cross-site scripting (XSS) attacks. To mitigate these risks, developers should adopt more secure storage solutions where available. On mobile platforms, leveraging secure key storage APIs, such as the iOS Keychain or Android Keystore, can help protect tokens. In SPAs, developers should prioritize securing the application against XSS and consider storing tokens only in memory, which reduces the attack surface by ensuring tokens are not persisted beyond the current session. While in-memory storage means tokens are lost on a page refresh, this tradeoff often results in stronger security.

In addition to storage concerns, public clients must also address the issue of token expiration and refresh. Short-lived access tokens help limit the window of opportunity for attackers if a token is stolen. However, since public clients often cannot securely store refresh tokens, they may need alternative approaches to maintain session continuity. For instance, SPAs can use silent reauthentication techniques by leveraging hidden iframes or background requests to the authorization server's authorization endpoint. By using a session cookie or other session-bound mechanism at the authorization server, the client can obtain a new access token without requiring the user to re-enter credentials, while still avoiding long-lived tokens. This approach balances usability and security, ensuring that users experience seamless logins without exposing sensitive tokens to prolonged risk.

CORS (Cross-Origin Resource Sharing) and secure headers also play an important role in protecting public clients, particularly SPAs. Since SPAs often communicate with APIs hosted on different domains, properly configured CORS headers on the API side ensure that only authorized origins can access the protected resources. Additionally, Content Security Policy (CSP) headers help prevent XSS attacks by restricting the sources from which scripts can be loaded. By carefully configuring CORS and CSP headers, developers can reduce the likelihood of unauthorized scripts or third-party sites accessing sensitive tokens.

Another consideration is the user's involvement and awareness. Public clients should clearly communicate to users which permissions they are requesting and why. Transparency builds trust and ensures that users are more likely to grant consent only when they understand what the application will do with their data. Moreover, providing users with easy ways to revoke tokens or sessions increases security. If a user suspects that their session or token has been compromised, they should be able to quickly revoke access without waiting for tokens to expire naturally. Offering users simple controls to manage their active sessions enhances both security and user experience.

In the broader security context, public clients must also remain vigilant against phishing attacks and malicious actors attempting to intercept tokens or credentials. Encouraging users to authenticate only through trusted, official login pages and educating them about the dangers of entering credentials on unknown sites can help mitigate these risks. Developers can further protect their applications by integrating multi-factor authentication (MFA) or device attestation checks, adding additional layers of security that make it harder for attackers to compromise user accounts or steal tokens.

Overall, public clients face inherent challenges due to their inability to securely store secrets, but these challenges can be mitigated through careful design and adherence to best practices. By leveraging PKCE, adopting secure token storage methods, using short-lived tokens and session-bound mechanisms, configuring secure headers, and maintaining transparency and user control, developers can protect public clients and ensure a more secure OAuth 2.0 implementation.

Building a Custom Authorization Server

A custom authorization server is a dedicated component that issues tokens, manages client applications, and enforces policies in an OAuth 2.0 ecosystem. While many organizations rely on established solutions like commercial identity providers or open-source platforms, others choose to build their own authorization servers to meet specific business requirements, integrate deeply with custom infrastructure, or maintain full control over the authorization process. Creating a custom authorization server involves careful planning, adherence to OAuth 2.0 standards, and a strong emphasis on security, scalability, and maintainability.

The foundation of any custom authorization server is its ability to issue and validate tokens. Access tokens serve as credentials that clients use to gain access to protected resources. In addition, ID tokens are often issued in OpenID Connect (OIDC) scenarios to convey user identity information. A well-designed authorization server must provide endpoints for obtaining these tokens, verifying them, and revoking them. The authorization endpoint allows users to authenticate and grant consent, while the token endpoint handles the exchange of authorization codes, client credentials, or other grants for tokens. The token introspection and revocation endpoints enable downstream services to confirm token validity and revoke tokens when needed. By implementing these endpoints according to OAuth 2.0 specifications, a custom authorization server ensures that it interoperates smoothly with clients and resource servers.

One of the key benefits of building a custom authorization server is the ability to tailor it to the organization's unique requirements. This might include integrating with proprietary user directories, supporting custom claims in tokens, or enforcing organization-specific policies. For instance, a company may need tokens that include detailed information about user roles, departments, or access levels. By customizing the token payload, the authorization server can provide exactly the information that downstream services need, reducing the need for additional lookups or API calls. This approach improves efficiency and simplifies the overall architecture while ensuring that security policies are consistently enforced at the point of token issuance.

Security is paramount when designing a custom authorization server. Token generation must be done using strong cryptographic algorithms, and all endpoints must be protected with TLS to prevent interception of credentials or tokens. The server should support multiple authentication methods, including password-based login, social logins, and multifactor authentication (MFA). For OIDC implementations, a discovery document should be provided, outlining the server's endpoints, supported scopes, signing algorithms, and public keys. By following best practices, such as regularly rotating signing keys and ensuring that tokens have appropriate expiration times, the custom authorization server can maintain a high level of trust and protect sensitive user data.

Client management is another critical aspect of building a custom authorization server. The server must provide a way for client applications to register, update, and delete their credentials. In traditional setups, this is often done manually through an administrative interface. However, implementing dynamic client registration allows clients to programmatically register and receive client IDs, reducing the overhead for administrators. The server must validate each client's information, assign appropriate scopes, and ensure that the client's redirect URIs are well-formed and properly registered. By enforcing strict validation and maintaining detailed records of registered clients, the authorization server helps prevent misuse and maintains the integrity of the authorization process.

The custom authorization server must also handle multiple grant types, as different scenarios call for different methods of obtaining tokens. The authorization code flow is ideal for server-based applications that can securely store client secrets, while the implicit flow (though less common in modern applications) historically catered to public clients like SPAs. The client credentials flow enables machine-to-machine communication, and the resource owner password credentials flow can be used in legacy scenarios. Supporting these flows ensures that the authorization server can accommodate a variety of client types and use cases, providing flexibility and scalability as the ecosystem evolves.

Performance and scalability are important considerations when building a custom authorization server. As the central component of the authorization ecosystem, the server must handle potentially high volumes of authorization requests, token exchanges, and introspection calls. Using a scalable infrastructure—such as containerized deployments, load balancing, and caching—ensures that the server remains responsive under heavy load. For example, caching the results of token introspection requests or using in-memory storage for frequently accessed keys can reduce latency and improve throughput.

By monitoring performance metrics, administrators can identify bottlenecks and make data-driven decisions to optimize the server's performance.

Another advantage of a custom authorization server is the ability to implement custom business logic and enforce complex policies. For example, the server can apply additional checks before issuing tokens, such as verifying that the user is in good standing, that certain prerequisites are met, or that the client's request aligns with the organization's governance rules. These custom policies help maintain a higher level of control over access to resources, ensuring that the authorization process aligns closely with the organization's strategic goals and compliance requirements.

Finally, thorough documentation and developer support are essential for a custom authorization server to succeed. Comprehensive API documentation, clear examples, and well-defined error messages help developers integrate their applications more easily and troubleshoot issues more effectively. Providing SDKs or client libraries for popular programming languages can further simplify adoption. The better the developer experience, the more smoothly client applications can be integrated and maintained, ultimately contributing to the long-term success of the custom authorization server.

In sum, building a custom authorization server allows organizations to address unique requirements, implement custom policies, and maintain full control over their authorization infrastructure. By following OAuth 2.0 standards, prioritizing security, and ensuring performance, scalability, and developer support, a custom authorization server can become a reliable and powerful cornerstone of an organization's identity and access management strategy.

OAuth 2.0 and the Zero Trust Model

The Zero Trust security model shifts the traditional perimeter-focused approach to one where trust is never assumed. Instead, every access request must be verified, authenticated, and authorized in real time, regardless of the request's origin or the resource being accessed. OAuth 2.0, as a flexible and well-established framework for securing APIs and applications, can play a vital role in supporting a Zero Trust strategy.

By providing strong authentication, granular authorization, and a consistent way to enforce policies, OAuth 2.0 helps ensure that access is granted only when certain conditions are met, aligning with the core principles of Zero Trust.

A key tenet of Zero Trust is the notion that every request must be authenticated and authorized, even if it originates from within the corporate network. OAuth 2.0 facilitates this by requiring clients to obtain tokens that represent the authorization granted by resource owners. When a client application or service requests access to a resource, it presents an access token that the resource server validates before fulfilling the request. This process ensures that only authorized entities can interact with protected resources, regardless of their network location. Because OAuth 2.0 tokens can be short-lived and scoped to specific permissions, they help maintain a minimal level of trust that must be continually re-evaluated, a core principle of the Zero Trust model.

Granular authorization is another area where OAuth 2.0 and Zero Trust principles align. In a Zero Trust environment, users and devices are given only the minimum permissions required to perform their tasks. OAuth 2.0's scope mechanism allows developers to define and enforce fine-grained access controls. For example, a token might be granted the ability to "read:profile" but not "write:profile," or "read:documents" for a specific project but not for the entire repository. By ensuring that each token carries only the permissions necessary for a particular operation, OAuth 2.0 reduces the risk of unauthorized access and limits the potential impact of compromised credentials. This approach supports the Zero Trust principle of least privilege, where no entity should have more access than it needs at any given time.

Dynamic context-aware policies are central to Zero Trust, and OAuth 2.0 provides a flexible framework to enforce them. Authorization servers can integrate with identity providers, policy engines, and contextual data sources to evaluate each request in real time. For instance, an authorization server might factor in device posture, user location, time of day, and behavioral patterns before issuing a token or allowing an access request. If a user's device is unpatched or a request originates from an unusual geographic location, the server can deny the token request, require additional authentication, or issue a token with reduced permissions. This real-time evaluation ensures that each access decision is based on the current security posture, which aligns perfectly with Zero Trust's demand for continuous verification.

Zero Trust also emphasizes the importance of monitoring and logging every access request. OAuth 2.0 naturally lends itself to detailed logging because every token issuance, validation, and revocation event can be captured. By maintaining comprehensive logs, organizations can track which users and devices accessed which resources, when, and under what conditions. This visibility not only helps detect anomalous behavior, but also supports incident response and compliance efforts. If a token is misused or an unexpected access pattern emerges, security teams can quickly investigate and take action. The ability to trace every access event back to a specific token or policy decision is a critical element of Zero Trust, and OAuth 2.0 provides the mechanisms needed to achieve it.

Another important aspect of Zero Trust is token revocation and rotation. Zero Trust requires that access can be revoked immediately if security conditions change. OAuth 2.0 supports this through token revocation endpoints, allowing administrators to invalidate access and refresh tokens as soon as a threat is detected. For example, if a user's device is reported as stolen or an account is compromised, the associated tokens can be revoked to prevent further access. In a Zero Trust model, this kind of immediate response is essential to maintaining a secure environment. OAuth 2.0's ability to issue short-lived tokens and refresh them only when necessary further strengthens this approach. By minimizing the lifetime of any given token, organizations can ensure that the access granted is always re-evaluated against current policies and conditions.

Device and user identity are key components of Zero Trust, and OAuth 2.0 integrates seamlessly with modern identity standards. OpenID Connect, which builds on OAuth 2.0, provides a standardized way to authenticate users and obtain identity claims. These claims can include information about the user's role, group membership, and authentication method, all of which can be used to enforce context-aware policies. By leveraging OpenID Connect, OAuth 2.0 becomes not just a framework for authorization but also a foundational piece of a broader Zero Trust identity strategy. This integration ensures that every access request is tied to a verified identity and evaluated in real time.

In Zero Trust architectures, APIs and microservices often serve as the backbone of application ecosystems. OAuth 2.0's ability to secure API endpoints through token-based authentication and authorization is critical in this context. By requiring tokens for every API call and validating them against the current security posture, OAuth 2.0 helps maintain Zero Trust principles at the application layer. Even if an attacker breaches one component, the consistent enforcement of token validation across all services prevents lateral movement and ensures that no resource is accessible without proper authorization. This continuous enforcement at every layer reinforces the Zero Trust approach, making it harder for attackers to exploit vulnerabilities or escalate privileges.

Ultimately, OAuth 2.0 provides the tools and flexibility needed to implement a robust Zero Trust model. By requiring authentication and authorization for every request, enforcing granular access controls, integrating real-time contextual policies, enabling detailed logging, and supporting immediate token revocation, OAuth 2.0 helps organizations transition to a security approach where trust is never assumed. This alignment with Zero Trust principles ensures that only authorized users and devices can access sensitive resources, regardless of their location or network environment.

Managing Multiple Resource Servers

As organizations adopt increasingly distributed and microservices-oriented architectures, the number of resource servers in their environment often grows. Each resource server, responsible for protecting and serving a particular set of APIs or data, must validate tokens and enforce authorization decisions. Managing multiple resource servers in an OAuth 2.0 ecosystem introduces unique challenges related to token validation, consistent policy enforcement, and scalability. By addressing these challenges effectively, developers and administrators can maintain secure and efficient access to resources across the entire environment.

One of the core tasks in managing multiple resource servers is ensuring that all servers share a consistent understanding of token validation. Each resource server must be able to verify that the tokens it receives are legitimate, have not been tampered with, and contain the necessary claims to grant access. In many implementations, tokens issued by the authorization server are JSON Web Tokens (JWTs) signed with a private key. Resource servers can then verify the signature using the corresponding public key, which can be fetched from the authorization server's published JSON Web Key Set (JWKS) endpoint. By relying on a common set of keys and standardized token claims, all resource servers can independently validate tokens without needing to call back to the authorization server for every request.

However, not all tokens are self-contained JWTs. In some cases, the authorization server issues opaque tokens that require introspection. Each resource server must know how to contact the introspection endpoint and authenticate its request to determine if a given token is active, what scopes it includes, and its expiration time. This setup can become complex as the number of resource servers increases. To streamline this process, administrators can use centralized libraries or shared services that handle introspection and token validation, ensuring that all resource servers follow the same validation logic. This approach reduces duplication and helps maintain a consistent security posture across the environment.

Scope management is another critical consideration when dealing with multiple resource servers. Different resource servers often require different sets of scopes to control access to their APIs. For example, a user profile API might define scopes like "read:profile" and "update:profile," while a payments API might have "read:transactions" and "process:payment" scopes. Ensuring that each resource server understands its relevant scopes and enforces them consistently is key to maintaining secure access control. The authorization server should issue tokens with clearly defined scopes, and each resource server must validate that the requested operation is allowed under the provided scopes. By standardizing scope definitions and ensuring that each server enforces them in the same way, organizations can prevent privilege escalation and maintain clear access boundaries.

Another challenge of managing multiple resource servers is handling token revocation and rotation. If a token is revoked or a signing key is rotated, all resource servers must be aware of the change as quickly as possible. For JWTs, this often involves regularly fetching the latest JWKS from the authorization server and verifying that the cached keys are still valid. For opaque tokens, resource servers need to perform introspection checks more frequently after a known revocation event. Using caching strategies and periodic refresh intervals helps resource servers stay up to date without overwhelming the authorization server. By automating these processes, administrators can ensure that all resource servers remain in sync and that invalid tokens are promptly rejected.

When scaling across multiple resource servers, performance and efficiency become crucial. Each resource server must handle potentially large volumes of token validation requests without introducing latency or bottlenecks. Implementing efficient caching strategies is one way to achieve this. For example, resource servers can cache validation results for short periods, reducing the frequency of introspection calls. They can also cache the public keys used for JWT signature verification, refreshing them only when the JWKS endpoint indicates that the keys have changed. These caching techniques help maintain responsiveness while ensuring that security checks are performed accurately and consistently.

Centralized policy management also plays an important role. As the number of resource servers grows, maintaining consistent authorization policies across all servers can become challenging. Introducing a centralized policy engine or an externalized access control system allows administrators to define policies in a single location and enforce them uniformly across multiple resource servers. By decoupling policy management from the resource servers themselves, organizations can ensure that changes are applied consistently and quickly without requiring updates to individual server configurations. This approach simplifies management, reduces configuration drift, and helps maintain a coherent security framework.

Monitoring and auditing are essential when managing multiple resource servers. By collecting detailed logs of token validation events, scope checks, and policy enforcement decisions, organizations gain visibility into how access is being granted and used. Centralized logging and analytics platforms can aggregate data from all resource servers, allowing security teams to identify patterns, detect anomalies, and respond to potential threats more effectively. This unified visibility is especially important in distributed environments where security incidents can span multiple services. With proper logging and monitoring, administrators can maintain a high level of security and quickly address issues as they arise.

As the environment evolves, regular reviews and updates to token handling procedures, scope definitions, and validation logic are necessary. Security standards and best practices change over time, and organizations must ensure that all resource servers are aligned with the latest recommendations. Periodic audits, code reviews, and compliance checks help maintain a secure and well-managed OAuth ecosystem, even as new resource servers are added or existing ones are retired.

Managing multiple resource servers in an OAuth 2.0 environment requires careful planning and coordination. By standardizing token validation, enforcing consistent scope definitions, automating key and token management processes, centralizing policy enforcement, and maintaining robust monitoring, organizations can create a scalable, secure, and efficient system for protecting resources. This approach ensures that all resource servers operate in harmony, providing reliable and consistent authorization throughout the entire ecosystem.

Logging and Auditing OAuth 2.0 Transactions

Logging and auditing OAuth 2.0 transactions are critical components of maintaining a secure and transparent authorization framework. As OAuth 2.0 is often used to protect sensitive resources, understanding how tokens are issued, validated, and used provides vital insights into the security and operational health of the system. A well-designed logging and auditing approach not only helps detect and respond to potential threats but also supports compliance, forensic investigations, and ongoing improvements to the authorization process.

Effective logging begins with identifying key events and activities that should be recorded. In an OAuth 2.0 environment, important events include token requests, authorization code exchanges, token validations, token refreshes, and token revocations. Each of these interactions represents a critical step in the authorization workflow, and capturing detailed logs at each stage helps maintain a complete and accurate picture of how access is granted and managed. For example, when a client requests an access token, the logs should include the client ID, the requested scopes, the IP address of the requestor, and the result of the request. Similarly, when a token is validated by a resource server, the logs should record the token's status, the resource being accessed, and any scope checks performed. By consistently capturing these data points, administrators gain visibility into the flow of tokens through the system and can quickly identify any deviations from normal patterns.

One of the primary goals of OAuth 2.0 logging is to detect and respond to anomalies. Abnormal activity, such as repeated token validation failures, an unusually high volume of refresh token exchanges, or multiple token revocation requests from the same client, can indicate potential security incidents. For instance, if a particular client ID is generating a large number of invalid token requests, it may suggest that the client's credentials have been compromised or that someone is attempting a brute force attack. With comprehensive logging in place, these anomalies can be identified in real time, and appropriate actions—such as revoking the client's access or investigating the source of the traffic—can be taken to mitigate the threat.

Auditing OAuth 2.0 transactions goes beyond real-time detection to provide a historical record of authorization and authentication activity. These records serve multiple purposes. First, they help ensure compliance with internal policies, regulatory requirements, and industry standards. Many compliance frameworks require organizations to demonstrate that access controls are enforced, that unauthorized access attempts are detected and addressed, and that privileged actions are monitored. Detailed audit logs provide the evidence needed to show that these requirements are met. Additionally, when an incident occurs, audit logs offer a timeline of events, helping security teams reconstruct what happened, determine the root cause, and implement corrective measures. Without reliable audit trails, understanding the scope and impact of a security breach becomes significantly more challenging.

Another benefit of logging and auditing OAuth 2.0 transactions is the ability to gain insights into system performance and usage trends. By analyzing logs over time, administrators can identify patterns such as peak usage periods, the most frequently requested scopes, or the most active clients. This data can inform decisions about scaling infrastructure, optimizing resource allocation, or refining access policies. For example, if logs reveal that certain clients consistently request more permissions than they use, administrators can adjust the default scopes granted to those clients, reducing the risk of over-permissioning and improving security. Similarly, usage data can guide investments in system capacity or inform changes to token expiration policies.

To make logging and auditing effective, organizations must implement consistent and reliable processes for collecting, storing, and analyzing log data. Logs should be centralized in a secure and scalable logging platform or a security information and event management (SIEM) system. Centralized logging allows administrators to correlate events across multiple components, such as authorization servers, resource servers, and client applications. It also simplifies the process of searching for specific events, generating reports, and setting up alerts. For example, if a token issued by the authorization server is used on multiple resource servers, a centralized log view helps track how that token is handled at each step, providing a clear end-to-end view of the transaction.

To maintain data integrity and ensure logs remain useful over time, organizations should implement log retention and archival policies. Logs that are retained for long enough periods support long-term trend analysis and provide historical context for future audits. However, retaining logs indefinitely may create unnecessary storage costs or introduce privacy concerns. By defining clear retention periods based on regulatory requirements, business needs, and security considerations, organizations can strike the right balance between accessibility and efficiency.

Finally, protecting the integrity and confidentiality of logs is essential. Since logs often contain sensitive information—such as client IDs, user identifiers, or token details—they must be stored securely. Access to log data should be restricted to authorized personnel, and strong encryption should be used to protect logs both at rest and in transit. Implementing role-based access controls, auditing log access attempts, and ensuring that all log-related operations are logged themselves further enhances the overall security of the logging system.

In summary, logging and auditing OAuth 2.0 transactions provide critical visibility into the authorization process, helping organizations maintain security, ensure compliance, and continuously improve their systems. By capturing key events, detecting anomalies, maintaining historical records, and using centralized and secure logging solutions, administrators can confidently manage their OAuth 2.0 ecosystem and respond effectively to any challenges that arise.

Compliance and Regulatory Considerations

Compliance and regulatory requirements significantly influence how OAuth 2.0 implementations are designed, deployed, and maintained. Organizations operating in regulated industries—such as finance, healthcare, or government—must ensure that their authentication and authorization processes meet stringent legal, industry, and internal policy standards. These requirements not only affect technical decisions, such as token lifetimes and logging practices, but also shape the broader approach to security, privacy, and data protection. By understanding the relevant compliance frameworks and adopting best practices, organizations can maintain a secure OAuth 2.0 environment while fulfilling their regulatory obligations.

One of the most well-known regulatory frameworks is the General Data Protection Regulation (GDPR), which applies to organizations that handle the personal data of individuals in the European Union. Under GDPR, companies must implement strong technical and organizational measures to protect user data, and they must provide transparency regarding how personal data is collected, processed, and stored. OAuth 2.0, as a standard for controlling access to user resources, plays a central role in ensuring compliance. For example, when designing an OAuth 2.0 authorization flow, organizations must clearly inform users about the scopes being requested and what data those scopes grant access to. This transparency helps fulfill GDPR's requirement for informed consent, allowing users to understand and control how their data is used.

Another critical consideration is token and credential security. Regulatory frameworks often mandate strict controls over sensitive data, including access tokens and refresh tokens. For instance, the Payment Card Industry Data Security Standard (PCI DSS) requires that sensitive authentication data be protected during transmission and storage. Although OAuth 2.0 tokens are not necessarily classified as payment data, organizations operating under PCI DSS must ensure that tokens cannot be intercepted, stolen, or misused to gain unauthorized access to cardholder data. To meet these requirements, OAuth 2.0 implementations must enforce secure communication channels, such as TLS, and adhere to strong encryption standards for stored tokens. In addition, using short-lived tokens and rotating keys frequently helps mitigate risks and align with compliance guidelines that emphasize minimizing the exposure of sensitive credentials.

Regulatory frameworks often include detailed logging and auditing requirements. For example, the Health Insurance Portability and Accountability Act (HIPAA) in the United States mandates that covered entities maintain audit trails of all access to protected health information (PHI). In the context of OAuth 2.0, this means that every token issuance, validation, and revocation must be logged in a way that supports accountability and traceability. Detailed logs must capture who accessed what data, when, and under what circumstances. By implementing robust logging practices, organizations can not only meet audit requirements but also provide evidence of compliance and help demonstrate that appropriate security controls are in place.

Identity and access management standards also play a role in regulatory compliance. The National Institute of Standards and Technology (NIST) publishes guidelines for digital identity and authentication, such as NIST Special Publication 800-63. Although NIST guidelines are not legally binding, they are widely adopted as best practices in government and private sector environments in the United States. NIST's recommendations include strong multifactor authentication, strict password policies, and secure handling of tokens.

By aligning OAuth 2.0 implementations with these guidelines, organizations can strengthen their security posture and improve their ability to comply with other regulatory requirements that reference NIST standards.

Privacy regulations often require organizations to minimize data collection and ensure that only authorized parties have access to user information. OAuth 2.0's scope mechanism supports these goals by allowing developers to request only the permissions they need. For example, instead of requesting broad access to all user data, an application can request access only to specific resources or actions, such as reading the user's email address or viewing their profile photo. By implementing granular scopes and enforcing least-privilege principles, organizations can reduce the risk of unauthorized access and demonstrate compliance with privacy regulations that emphasize data minimization and purpose limitation.

Key management practices are another area where compliance requirements intersect with OAuth 2.0. Regulatory standards often mandate that cryptographic keys used to sign or encrypt tokens be rotated regularly, stored securely, and monitored for unauthorized access. OAuth 2.0 implementations that rely on JSON Web Tokens (JWTs) must carefully manage the signing keys, ensuring that private keys are stored in secure hardware modules or dedicated key management systems. These measures not only protect against key compromise but also help meet compliance standards that require strong cryptographic controls.

Data residency and sovereignty requirements also come into play, especially for organizations operating in multiple jurisdictions. Certain regulations require that user data, including tokens and logs, be stored within specific geographic regions. OAuth 2.0 implementations must account for these restrictions by ensuring that tokens are issued and validated in compliance with local data residency laws. For example, an organization might operate multiple authorization servers in different regions, each configured to store tokens and logs within the respective country's boundaries. By designing the system to respect data residency requirements, organizations can remain compliant while continuing to leverage OAuth 2.0's capabilities.

Finally, compliance is not a one-time effort. As regulations evolve and new standards emerge, organizations must continuously review and update their OAuth 2.0 implementations. Regular compliance assessments, audits, and penetration tests help identify potential gaps and ensure that the environment remains secure and in line with regulatory expectations. By integrating compliance considerations into the design, deployment, and maintenance of OAuth 2.0 systems, organizations can meet their regulatory obligations while maintaining a secure and user-friendly authorization infrastructure.

Extending OAuth 2.0: Custom Grant Types

OAuth 2.0 provides a flexible and extensible framework for authorization, offering several standardized grant types that cater to a wide range of common use cases. However, not all scenarios fit neatly into the predefined flows like authorization code, client credentials, or implicit grant types. When organizations encounter unique authentication and authorization requirements, custom grant types can be introduced to extend the functionality of OAuth 2.0 without breaking its core principles. By carefully designing and implementing custom grant types, developers can address specialized use cases, integrate legacy systems, and meet complex business needs while still leveraging the strengths of the OAuth 2.0 protocol.

A custom grant type is essentially a new way for a client application to obtain an access token from the authorization server. Instead of relying on the standard set of parameters and flows defined in the OAuth 2.0 specification, a custom grant type allows the client to present alternative credentials or proofs of authorization. The authorization server recognizes this custom grant and responds accordingly, issuing tokens based on the organization's specific policies and requirements. The key advantage of custom grants is their ability to integrate seamlessly with the existing OAuth framework, enabling organizations to maintain a unified approach to token issuance, validation, and management.

One common scenario where custom grant types are beneficial is when integrating with legacy authentication systems. Many organizations have long-established identity stores or authentication methods that predate OAuth 2.0. For example, a company might still use a proprietary single sign-on (SSO) solution or an older form of token-based authentication. By defining a custom grant type, the organization can bridge the gap between the legacy system and its modern OAuth 2.0 ecosystem. The custom grant can allow the client to present a legacy token or a custom credential, which the authorization server verifies against the legacy system before issuing a standard OAuth access token. This approach enables the organization to continue leveraging its existing infrastructure while gradually transitioning to a more modern, standards-based architecture.

Another use case for custom grant types involves scenarios where additional security requirements must be enforced. For instance, a highly sensitive application might require a second layer of verification beyond the standard authorization code flow. A custom grant type could be created to include additional authentication factors, such as a one-time password (OTP), a biometric confirmation, or a device attestation. In this case, the client would provide not only the authorization code but also the additional proof of identity required by the custom grant. The authorization server validates these extra factors before issuing the token, providing a more secure authorization process tailored to the organization's needs.

Custom grant types can also help streamline complex workflows that involve multiple parties or services. In some business scenarios, the traditional grant types may not easily accommodate workflows where a token needs to be exchanged for additional privileges or transferred between services. A custom grant type can be designed to handle these unique workflows by incorporating additional context, such as the specific resource being accessed, the user's relationship to multiple organizations, or a chain of delegation. By encoding this context into the custom grant, the authorization server can issue tokens that reflect the precise permissions and constraints required, ensuring that each party in the workflow only gains access to the appropriate resources.

One important consideration when implementing custom grant types is to maintain consistency with the core OAuth 2.0 model. The authorization server should continue to issue tokens using standard formats, such as JSON Web Tokens (JWTs), and adhere to established token validation and revocation processes. This ensures that resource servers and downstream services can handle tokens in the same way, regardless of how they were obtained. In other words, the custom grant type should only affect the initial issuance of the token, leaving the broader OAuth ecosystem untouched. By doing so, the organization can extend the protocol without introducing complexity or breaking interoperability.

Another key factor is ensuring that custom grant types are thoroughly documented and well-understood by all parties involved. Since custom grants are not part of the standard OAuth specification, client developers and resource server implementers must have clear guidance on how to use them. Providing detailed documentation, including the parameters required, the validation logic, and the expected token formats, helps ensure smooth integration and reduces the likelihood of errors. Furthermore, organizations should consider versioning their custom grants and maintaining backward compatibility when possible. This allows for incremental improvements and adaptations without disrupting existing integrations.

Security is paramount when extending OAuth 2.0 with custom grant types. Since custom grants often involve handling non-standard credentials or additional context, the authorization server must implement rigorous validation checks. All inputs should be sanitized and verified, and any third-party authentication or data sources should be trusted and reliable. The authorization server should also perform robust logging and monitoring of custom grant requests, allowing administrators to detect unusual patterns, investigate anomalies, and respond to potential threats quickly. By applying the same level of security rigor to custom grants as to standard ones, organizations can maintain the integrity of their OAuth 2.0 environment.

Custom grant types are a powerful way to extend OAuth 2.0 to meet unique and specialized requirements. By carefully designing and documenting these grants, integrating them with existing workflows, and maintaining strict security practices, organizations can address their most complex use cases without compromising the stability or interoperability of their OAuth ecosystem. Through thoughtful implementation, custom grant types enable organizations to fully leverage the flexibility and power of OAuth 2.0 while ensuring a seamless and secure experience for users and developers alike.

Migrating from Legacy Authentication Protocols

As organizations increasingly adopt modern security standards, many face the challenge of migrating from legacy authentication protocols to more robust frameworks like OAuth 2.0. Legacy protocols—such as HTTP Basic Authentication, proprietary token schemes, or older single sign-on (SSO) solutions—often lack the flexibility, security, and scalability required in today's complex digital ecosystems. Moving to OAuth 2.0 offers significant advantages, including enhanced security, standardized token handling, and improved support for distributed and cloud-native applications. However, making this transition requires careful planning, a clear understanding of the differences between protocols, and a structured approach to minimize disruptions and risks.

The first step in migrating away from legacy authentication protocols is understanding the limitations of the current system. Older protocols often rely on static credentials, such as shared secrets or passwords, that are transmitted with every request. These static credentials can be easily intercepted if not properly encrypted, and they offer no inherent mechanism for fine-grained access control or scope-based permissions. Additionally, legacy protocols may lack support for modern identity federation or multi-factor authentication, making it difficult to integrate with new identity providers or meet evolving security standards. Identifying these limitations provides a strong foundation for justifying the migration and helps guide the selection of appropriate OAuth 2.0 features to implement.

Next, it's essential to analyze the existing workflows and use cases. Understanding how users and applications currently authenticate and access resources is critical for designing an equivalent—or better— experience with OAuth 2.0. For example, if a legacy system uses a proprietary token format to grant access to APIs, you'll need to determine how to replace that token issuance and validation process with OAuth 2.0 tokens. This might involve defining OAuth 2.0 scopes that align with the existing permissions model, identifying the appropriate grant types (such as authorization code flow or client credentials flow), and mapping legacy roles and entitlements to OAuth

2.0 claims. By thoroughly documenting these workflows and mappings, you can ensure that the new system will meet all current requirements while also providing a foundation for future improvements.

One of the most significant changes when migrating to OAuth 2.0 is adopting a token-based model for authentication and authorization. Instead of relying on a single shared credential or a proprietary token, OAuth 2.0 introduces access tokens and optionally refresh tokens. Access tokens are issued by an authorization server and contain the information resource servers need to verify the requester's identity and permissions. This approach not only standardizes how tokens are issued, validated, and managed, but also enables the use of short-lived tokens. By limiting token lifetimes and using refresh tokens to obtain new ones, organizations reduce the impact of token compromise and strengthen their overall security posture. Transitioning from static credentials to this dynamic token model may require updating application logic, integrating with a new authorization server, and ensuring that resource servers are prepared to validate tokens according to the OAuth 2.0 specification.

Security is a primary driver for migrating from legacy authentication protocols, and OAuth 2.0 provides several critical enhancements. For example, OAuth 2.0 enforces the use of secure transport (TLS) for all communication, protecting tokens and credentials from interception. In addition, the standard encourages the use of strong cryptographic algorithms and supports advanced security features such as Proof Key for Code Exchange (PKCE) and token introspection. By integrating these features, organizations can address many of the vulnerabilities inherent in legacy systems, such as token replay attacks, credential leaks, and inadequate access controls. As part of the migration process, security teams should review existing threat models and implement the necessary safeguards to fully leverage OAuth 2.0's capabilities.

Another important aspect of migration is ensuring a seamless transition for users and clients. If the existing system supports numerous applications, developers need to be involved early in the process to understand the changes, update their integration points, and test new flows. Providing clear documentation, SDKs, and sample code helps developers adapt their applications more quickly. Similarly, end-users should experience minimal disruption. For instance, maintaining existing user accounts, mapping roles and permissions directly to OAuth 2.0 scopes or claims, and offering self-service tools for managing tokens can help users transition smoothly. Clear communication about the benefits of the new system—such as stronger security, better integration with modern apps, and more granular control over data—can also encourage adoption and reduce resistance.

The migration process itself often involves running the legacy and OAuth 2.0 systems in parallel for a time. This dual-mode operation allows organizations to test the new OAuth 2.0 implementation without immediately deprecating the legacy protocol. By gradually migrating clients and users, administrators can monitor for issues, gather feedback, and fine-tune the new system before fully retiring the legacy infrastructure. During this phase, logging and auditing are crucial. Detailed logs help identify unexpected errors, misconfigurations, or security concerns, allowing for timely adjustments. Once the new system proves stable and reliable, the legacy protocol can be phased out entirely, reducing maintenance overhead and eliminating outdated security risks.

Ultimately, migrating from legacy authentication protocols to OAuth 2.0 is not just a technical upgrade—it's an opportunity to modernize the organization's entire approach to identity and access management. By embracing OAuth 2.0's standardized, flexible, and secure framework, organizations can address existing vulnerabilities, improve interoperability with modern platforms, and position themselves for future growth and innovation.

OAuth 2.0 in Federation and Identity Federation

In today's interconnected digital environment, organizations frequently rely on identity federation to enable seamless, secure access across multiple domains, applications, and organizations. Identity federation involves linking user identities from one trusted entity, such as an enterprise identity provider, to another, such as a third-party application or service provider. By establishing trust relationships between these entities, users can authenticate once and gain access to resources in different systems without having to log in separately each time. OAuth 2.0, as a flexible and widely adopted authorization framework, plays a vital role in making identity federation secure, scalable, and user-friendly.

At the heart of identity federation is the concept of a federation trust. This trust is established between identity providers (IdPs), which manage user credentials and authentication, and service providers (SPs), which host applications and resources. Traditionally, federation protocols like SAML (Security Assertion Markup Language) have been used to implement these trust relationships. However, OAuth 2.0, often in combination with OpenID Connect (OIDC), has emerged as a modern alternative that supports simpler integrations, a broader range of client types, and better compatibility with mobile and cloud-based applications. OAuth 2.0 provides a framework for delegating authorization decisions to a central IdP, enabling service providers to rely on that trusted IdP for authenticating users and issuing tokens.

In a federated environment, OAuth 2.0 acts as the foundation for issuing and validating access tokens that enable users to access resources across multiple systems. When a user attempts to access a federated application, the application redirects them to the central IdP's authorization server. The user authenticates with the IdP, and upon successful authentication, the IdP issues an authorization code that the application exchanges for an access token. This access token is then used to make API calls or request data from other federated services. Because the access token is issued by a trusted IdP, all participating service providers can rely on it to validate user requests, enforce policies, and maintain a consistent user experience across the federation.

One of the key advantages of using OAuth 2.0 in federation is its ability to handle a wide variety of clients and platforms. Traditional federation protocols often required significant overhead to set up, maintain, and integrate with newer environments like mobile apps or single-page applications (SPAs). OAuth 2.0, by contrast, was designed with modern development paradigms in mind. It offers standardized flows, such as the authorization code flow and the implicit flow, that can be adapted to different client types. This flexibility makes it easier to incorporate mobile applications, SPAs, and IoT devices into a federated identity ecosystem. By using OAuth 2.0, organizations can extend their federated identity model beyond legacy web applications, creating a more seamless and consistent experience for users across all devices and platforms.

Another important benefit of OAuth 2.0 in identity federation is its compatibility with OpenID Connect. OpenID Connect builds on OAuth 2.0 by adding a standardized layer for user authentication. While OAuth 2.0 is focused primarily on authorization—granting access to resources—OpenID Connect introduces the concept of ID tokens, which contain identity-related claims about the authenticated user. This integration allows federated systems to handle both authentication and authorization in a unified way. When a user authenticates through the IdP, they receive an ID token that confirms their identity and an access token that allows them to access resources. Service providers within the federation can then use the ID token to identify the user and the access token to enforce fine-grained access controls. The combination of OAuth 2.0 and OpenID Connect streamlines the implementation of identity federation and simplifies the process of linking identities across multiple organizations.

Security is a primary concern in any federated identity scenario, and OAuth 2.0 provides several mechanisms to ensure that tokens are handled safely. Access tokens can be short-lived, reducing the risk if a token is compromised. Refresh tokens can be used to obtain new access tokens without requiring the user to reauthenticate, improving the user experience while maintaining security. OAuth 2.0 also supports features like Proof Key for Code Exchange (PKCE), which enhances the authorization code flow by adding an additional layer of protection against code interception. By leveraging these security features, organizations can confidently use OAuth 2.0 to establish and maintain trust within their identity federation.

In addition to securing tokens, OAuth 2.0 facilitates granular access control through scopes. Scopes define what actions a token permits and which resources it can access. This granularity is particularly valuable in federated environments where multiple service providers offer different sets of APIs and resources. By assigning specific scopes to each token, the IdP ensures that the user only has access to the resources they need, in line with the policies of the federation. This level of control helps prevent over-permissioning and ensures that access is both secure and appropriate for each user's role and responsibilities.

Another critical aspect of OAuth 2.0 in federation is the ability to support multiple IdPs and cross-domain trust relationships. Large federations often involve several independent IdPs, each managing their own user base. OAuth 2.0 supports the discovery and configuration of multiple authorization servers, enabling a seamless experience for users regardless of which IdP they belong to. By using a shared token format, such as JSON Web Tokens (JWTs), and standard validation mechanisms, all service providers in the federation can verify tokens issued by different IdPs. This interoperability ensures that users can move freely within the federation while maintaining a consistent and secure authentication and authorization experience.

Overall, OAuth 2.0's flexibility, security features, and compatibility with modern development practices make it a powerful tool for implementing identity federation. By enabling centralized trust, granular access control, and seamless user experiences across multiple domains, OAuth 2.0 helps organizations establish and maintain federated identity systems that are secure, scalable, and well-suited to the demands of today's digital landscape.

Delegation and Consent Management

Delegation and consent management are fundamental components of any robust OAuth 2.0 implementation. These concepts ensure that users remain in control of their data and can make informed decisions about how their information is shared and used. By enabling users to delegate access to specific resources and manage their consent for data sharing, OAuth 2.0 supports a transparent, user-centered approach to authorization that fosters trust and reduces the risk of misuse or over-permissioning.

Delegation in OAuth 2.0 allows users to grant limited access to their data without sharing their credentials. Instead of directly providing a username and password to a third-party application, users can authorize the application to act on their behalf by issuing it an access token. This token is scoped to a defined set of permissions, ensuring that the application can only access the data or perform the actions explicitly approved by the user. This model not only protects user credentials but also provides a clear boundary for what the delegated application can and cannot do, reducing the likelihood of accidental or malicious overreach.

Consent management is closely tied to delegation and plays a critical role in ensuring that users are fully aware of and comfortable with the level of access they grant. In an OAuth 2.0 flow, when a user attempts to sign in or connect a third-party application, they are presented with a consent screen. This screen lists the scopes being requested by the application, such as the ability to read profile information, view email addresses, or access calendar events. By reviewing these scopes, the user can make an informed decision about whether to allow or deny access. The consent process empowers users by making them active participants in the authorization process, rather than passive recipients of default permissions.

One of the challenges of managing delegation and consent is ensuring that the scopes requested by the application align with the actual needs of the application. Overly broad scopes can lead to unnecessary risk, while overly narrow scopes can hinder functionality. For example, if an application requests write access to all of a user's data when it only needs read access to a specific resource, the user may hesitate to grant access or feel their privacy is being unnecessarily compromised. To address this, developers must carefully define the scopes they request and ensure that each scope corresponds to a genuine need. Providing clear, concise descriptions of what each scope allows helps users understand the implications of their choices, making them more likely to provide informed consent.

Consent management also involves maintaining a record of what access has been granted and providing users with tools to review, revoke, or update their choices. This can be achieved through a centralized user dashboard or a similar interface where users can view a list of all connected applications, the scopes they have approved, and the dates of their last use. By offering users the ability to easily revoke tokens or update permissions, the system maintains transparency and trust. This ongoing control helps ensure that users feel confident in their ability to manage their own data and reduces the risk of lingering permissions that are no longer needed or appropriate.

Another aspect of effective consent management is the ability to handle changes in authorization requirements over time. Applications may evolve, requiring additional permissions or relinquishing previously needed access. In such cases, the consent management system must prompt users to reapprove the new scopes before they take effect. This ensures that users remain informed and that the principle of least privilege is consistently applied. By implementing a process that prompts users for consent whenever access requirements change, organizations can maintain a secure and transparent authorization framework that respects user autonomy.

From a technical perspective, implementing delegation and consent management requires a well-structured authorization server and a thoughtful approach to user experience. The authorization server must enforce scope restrictions and ensure that only approved tokens can access protected resources. It must also provide endpoints that allow resource servers to verify tokens, ensuring that the permissions encoded in the token match the user's original consent. On the user experience side, clear, concise consent screens, transparent descriptions of requested scopes, and an easy-to-use dashboard for reviewing and managing permissions are key to fostering user trust and engagement.

Security is a critical consideration in delegation and consent management. When users delegate access to an application, the resulting access token must be properly secured to prevent unauthorized use. Using short-lived tokens, refreshing them only when necessary, and ensuring that tokens are stored securely reduces the risk of token theft. Additionally, implementing secure communication channels, such as TLS, and enforcing strict validation of token claims help maintain the integrity of the delegation process. These security measures, combined with transparent consent management, ensure that users can trust the system to protect their data and uphold their choices.

In summary, delegation and consent management are essential for creating a secure, user-centered OAuth 2.0 ecosystem. By enabling users to grant limited access to their data, carefully defining scopes, providing transparent consent interfaces, and maintaining robust security measures, organizations can build trust, ensure compliance, and reduce the risk of data misuse. As applications and user expectations continue to evolve, a strong focus on delegation and consent management will remain a cornerstone of effective OAuth 2.0 implementations.

Token-Based Authentication Patterns

Token-based authentication has become a standard approach for securing modern applications and APIs. Unlike traditional session-based methods, where user authentication state is maintained on the server side, token-based authentication relies on the client presenting a token—a compact, self-contained piece of information that represents the user's identity and permissions—with each request. This method offers greater flexibility, scalability, and a cleaner separation of concerns. By examining common token-based authentication patterns, developers can understand when and how to apply these techniques, ensuring that their systems are both secure and user-friendly.

One of the most widely used patterns is the bearer token pattern. In this approach, the client includes an access token in the Authorization header of each HTTP request. The resource server validates the token to determine whether the request is authorized. If the token is valid and contains the required permissions, the server grants access to the requested resource. Bearer tokens are straightforward to implement, as they do not require the server to maintain any session state. Instead, all the necessary information is embedded within the token itself or can be retrieved using the token. This simplicity makes the bearer token pattern particularly suitable for APIs and microservices, where statelessness is a key architectural goal.

Another common pattern involves the use of refresh tokens alongside access tokens. Access tokens are typically short-lived to minimize the risk of misuse if they are compromised. However, requiring users to log in frequently can degrade the user experience. Refresh tokens address this issue by allowing the client to request a new access token without prompting the user for credentials again. This pattern is particularly useful in long-lived sessions or environments where continuous user interaction is expected, such as web applications or mobile apps. By securely storing the refresh token and exchanging it for new access tokens, the client maintains a seamless experience for the user while still adhering to security best practices.

The token exchange pattern is another variation often seen in distributed architectures. This pattern involves swapping one token for another with different properties or scopes. For example, a client application might receive a token that allows it to perform high-level operations. When it needs to interact with a more restricted microservice, it exchanges the original token for one that only permits the specific actions required by that service. This pattern supports the principle of least privilege by ensuring that each component of the system operates only with the permissions it truly needs. It also reduces the risk associated with a token compromise, as any stolen token is only valid within a narrowly defined scope.

Token chaining is a related pattern that applies in multi-service environments. Here, a token is passed through multiple layers of services, with each service validating the token and potentially adding its own claims or context. For instance, a request might originate from a frontend client, go through a gateway service, and then be forwarded to several backend microservices. Each service along the chain validates the token's authenticity and checks its claims to ensure that the requested action is permitted. This pattern ensures that the token remains the single source of truth for authorization decisions, allowing each service to act independently while maintaining consistent security policies.

In addition to these patterns, developers can also implement token introspection. Introspection involves querying the authorization server to verify the validity of a token and retrieve additional metadata, such as its expiration time, scopes, or associated user. This pattern is useful when tokens are opaque or when the resource server does not have the means to directly validate tokens on its own. By relying on the authorization server's introspection endpoint, the resource server ensures that every token it processes is still valid and meets the required security criteria. This centralized approach can simplify token management, especially in environments with multiple resource servers or frequently rotating tokens.

Another token-based authentication pattern is the use of structured tokens, such as JSON Web Tokens (JWTs). JWTs are self-contained tokens that include a set of claims, a signature, and, optionally, an encrypted payload. The claims might contain user identifiers, roles, scopes, and other metadata. Resource servers can verify the JWT's signature using a known public key, allowing them to trust the token without contacting the authorization server. This pattern reduces latency and improves performance, as tokens can be validated locally. However, it also requires careful key management and secure handling of token payloads to prevent tampering or leakage.

The choice of token pattern often depends on the specific requirements of the application. Factors such as the number of services, the need for fine-grained access control, the frequency of token rotation, and the sensitivity of the data being protected all influence which pattern is most appropriate. For instance, a single-page application (SPA) that interacts with a few backend APIs might rely on short-lived bearer tokens combined with refresh tokens. In contrast, a large microservices architecture might implement token chaining and token exchange to ensure that each service operates with minimal privileges.

When designing token-based authentication, it is crucial to consider security best practices. Tokens must be stored securely on the client side and transmitted only over secure channels, such as HTTPS. Implementing short token lifetimes, rotating signing keys regularly, and using secure algorithms for token signing and encryption help mitigate risks. Additionally, clear documentation of token lifecycles, scopes, and expiration policies ensures that all stakeholders understand how tokens are managed and what steps to take in the event of a token compromise.

Token-based authentication patterns offer powerful tools for building scalable, secure, and efficient authentication and authorization systems. By selecting the right pattern and following established best practices, developers can provide robust protection for their applications and APIs while delivering a seamless experience for users.

OAuth 2.0 in IoT Environments

The proliferation of Internet of Things (IoT) devices has introduced a host of new challenges for authentication, authorization, and security. IoT environments often include a wide array of devices with varying capabilities, ranging from low-power sensors and cameras to more sophisticated gateways and edge computing nodes. Many of these devices need to access cloud resources, communicate with one another, or send data to central platforms, all of which require a secure mechanism to control access. OAuth 2.0, while originally designed for more traditional web and mobile applications, provides a flexible framework that can be adapted to meet the unique needs of IoT deployments.

One of the primary considerations when applying OAuth 2.0 in IoT environments is the limited computational and storage resources of many IoT devices. While a typical web application can handle cryptographic operations and store secrets securely, a battery-powered sensor or embedded device might lack the hardware acceleration or secure storage needed for complex authentication flows. In such cases, careful selection of grant types and token lifetimes is essential. For example, devices that can store a pre-shared key might use the client credentials flow to authenticate directly to an authorization server, while devices without secure storage might rely on alternative methods, such as using a trusted gateway to obtain tokens on their behalf.

A common pattern in IoT is the use of a gateway or edge device that acts as an intermediary between low-power devices and the broader network. These gateways can handle the more computationally intensive aspects of OAuth 2.0, such as obtaining and refreshing tokens, and then distribute short-lived access tokens to the devices that need them. By offloading the heavy lifting to gateways, IoT environments can maintain a secure token-based system even when the individual devices themselves are not capable of running full OAuth 2.0 flows. This approach also simplifies device onboarding and management, as the gateway can be pre-configured with client credentials and scopes, ensuring consistent policies across the entire IoT deployment.

Another consideration in IoT environments is the need for fine-grained access control. IoT devices often interact with multiple services or resources, and not all devices should have the same level of access. OAuth 2.0's scope mechanism allows administrators to define granular permissions that align with each device's role. For instance, a temperature sensor might only need read access to a specific data ingestion endpoint, while a gateway device might have additional privileges to send configuration updates. By assigning different scopes to tokens, organizations can enforce least privilege principles, minimizing the potential impact of a compromised device or token.

Token lifetimes and refresh strategies are also critical in IoT. Short-lived access tokens reduce the window of opportunity for attackers if a token is intercepted or leaked. However, frequently refreshing tokens can be impractical for devices that are frequently offline or operate in remote locations with intermittent connectivity. In such cases, it's important to balance security and practicality. One approach is to use long-lived refresh tokens that can be securely stored on more capable devices, such as gateways, while the IoT endpoints themselves rely on short-lived tokens issued by the gateway. When a refresh is needed, the gateway can contact the authorization server to obtain a new access token, even if the endpoint device remains offline.

IoT environments also often require robust logging and monitoring. By recording every token issuance, validation, and revocation event, administrators gain insight into how devices are interacting with the system. This logging data can be used to detect anomalies, identify potential security incidents, and ensure that access policies are being enforced correctly. For example, if a specific device suddenly begins requesting tokens at an unusual frequency or attempts to access resources outside its assigned scope, these patterns can be flagged and investigated. A strong logging and monitoring strategy helps maintain the integrity of the OAuth 2.0 deployment and provides the visibility needed to respond quickly to potential threats.

Another challenge in IoT is handling device onboarding and identity management. OAuth 2.0 can be integrated with device provisioning systems to streamline the process. When a new device is introduced into the environment, it can be issued an initial token or set of credentials that allow it to register itself with the authorization server.

This initial registration process might involve a combination of manufacturer-provided credentials, device serial numbers, or hardware-based keys. Once registered, the device can request access tokens as needed, using a well-defined flow that aligns with the organization's security policies. By incorporating OAuth 2.0 into the onboarding process, organizations ensure that every device is accounted for and that all communications are protected from the start.

Finally, interoperability and standardization are important considerations in IoT environments. IoT ecosystems often include devices and platforms from multiple vendors, each with its own protocols and security models. By using OAuth 2.0, organizations can adopt a widely accepted standard that simplifies integration and reduces the complexity of managing disparate systems. OAuth 2.0's token-based model provides a consistent way to handle authentication and authorization across different types of devices and services, ensuring that all components of the IoT deployment can securely communicate without custom, vendor-specific solutions.

Overall, OAuth 2.0 offers a flexible framework that can be adapted to address the unique challenges of IoT environments. By leveraging its token-based model, scope-based access control, and support for various grant types, organizations can create secure, scalable, and manageable IoT systems. Although the constrained nature of many IoT devices requires thoughtful implementation, OAuth 2.0 provides a solid foundation for securing interactions, enforcing policies, and maintaining trust throughout the IoT ecosystem.

Authentication for Multi-Tenant Systems

Multi-tenant systems present unique challenges when it comes to authentication. In a multi-tenant architecture, a single instance of an application or platform is used to serve multiple, distinct tenants— often represented by different organizations or groups of users. While this approach improves resource utilization and simplifies infrastructure management, it also introduces complexities in ensuring that users are authenticated and authorized correctly, without accidentally exposing one tenant's data to another. Effective authentication strategies for multi-tenant systems require careful planning, robust identity management, and flexible security configurations.

One of the first considerations in authenticating users in a multi-tenant system is how to differentiate between tenants. Each tenant typically has its own set of users, roles, and permissions. When a user attempts to log in, the system must determine which tenant they belong to so it can authenticate them against the correct identity store or policy set. This process often involves capturing a tenant identifier early in the authentication flow. The tenant identifier can be derived from various factors, such as the subdomain the user is accessing, a custom domain assigned to the tenant, or a unique parameter provided during login. Once the system identifies the tenant, it can direct the user's authentication request to the appropriate identity provider or database.

Another important factor is managing tenant-specific identity providers. In many multi-tenant scenarios, each tenant may prefer or require a different identity provider, such as an enterprise's internal Active Directory, a corporate single sign-on solution, or a social login provider. To support these variations, the authentication system must be able to dynamically select and integrate with multiple identity providers. This often involves using a federated identity approach, where the multi-tenant system acts as a relying party or service provider, and the tenant's chosen identity provider serves as the identity authority. By supporting standards like SAML, OpenID Connect, or OAuth 2.0, the system can enable seamless integration with a wide range of identity providers, allowing tenants to use their existing infrastructure while maintaining a consistent authentication experience.

Role and permission management also plays a crucial role in authentication for multi-tenant systems. Once a user's identity is established, the system must determine their roles within their specific tenant and grant access accordingly. In a multi-tenant architecture, it is essential to ensure that these roles are strictly scoped to the tenant. A user who is an administrator in one tenant should not have administrative privileges in another tenant unless explicitly granted. To achieve this isolation, roles and permissions are typically tied to a tenant identifier, and all authorization decisions incorporate tenant-aware logic. This ensures that even if a user account exists in multiple tenants, their roles and permissions are managed separately, reducing the risk of cross-tenant privilege escalation.

Another key consideration is how to handle authentication flows that vary by tenant. Different tenants may have different security requirements, such as requiring multi-factor authentication (MFA), setting stricter password policies, or mandating periodic reauthentication. The authentication system must be flexible enough to accommodate these tenant-specific policies. For example, one tenant might integrate with a hardware-based MFA solution, while another tenant might prefer a software-based OTP mechanism. The system should be capable of enforcing these policies without requiring changes to the underlying application code. A common approach is to maintain tenant-specific configurations in a centralized directory or database, allowing the authentication logic to adapt dynamically based on the tenant's requirements.

Scalability is also a critical aspect of authentication for multi-tenant systems. As the number of tenants and users grows, the authentication system must be able to handle increasing authentication requests without performance degradation. This often involves implementing caching strategies, optimizing database queries, and distributing authentication workloads across multiple servers or regions. Additionally, ensuring high availability is crucial—any downtime in the authentication service can impact all tenants simultaneously. By designing the authentication layer to be resilient and scalable, organizations can provide a consistent experience to all tenants regardless of size or usage patterns.

Security considerations are paramount in a multi-tenant environment. Because multiple tenants share the same underlying infrastructure, it is essential to isolate authentication data and processes at every level. This includes encrypting sensitive information, such as credentials and tokens, both at rest and in transit. It also involves implementing strict access controls so that only authorized personnel can manage tenant configurations or view tenant-specific logs. Regular security audits, vulnerability assessments, and compliance checks help ensure that the authentication system remains robust and resistant to attacks.

Monitoring and logging are vital for maintaining visibility into authentication events across all tenants. Centralized logging allows administrators to track login attempts, authentication failures, and other security-related events. By correlating these logs with tenant identifiers, it becomes possible to identify patterns, such as a sudden increase in failed logins for a particular tenant, which might indicate a targeted attack. With appropriate monitoring and alerting in place, the authentication team can quickly respond to potential threats and maintain the integrity of the multi-tenant system.

Lastly, providing tenants with self-service management capabilities can improve the overall authentication experience. Tenants should be able to configure their identity provider integrations, define custom authentication policies, and manage their users and roles through a dedicated portal or dashboard. This approach reduces the administrative burden on the platform provider and empowers tenants to tailor the authentication experience to their specific needs. By offering these self-service tools, the system can accommodate a diverse range of tenant requirements while maintaining a standardized, secure foundation for authentication.

In summary, authentication in multi-tenant systems requires a combination of tenant-aware identity management, flexible role-based access control, support for multiple identity providers, and robust security measures. By implementing a scalable, configurable, and tenant-focused authentication strategy, organizations can ensure that each tenant's users are authenticated securely, their data remains isolated, and their experience meets the highest standards of reliability and performance.

Integrating OAuth 2.0 with Existing IAM Solutions

Integrating OAuth 2.0 with existing Identity and Access Management (IAM) solutions is a critical step for organizations looking to modernize their authentication and authorization infrastructure without disrupting established workflows. Many organizations have already invested significant resources in their IAM platforms, which often include directories like Active Directory, identity federation solutions, or proprietary single sign-on (SSO) implementations. By extending these systems to support OAuth 2.0, organizations can enable more flexible, standards-based access control for their APIs, mobile applications, and cloud services while preserving their existing investments in identity and policy management.

The first step in integrating OAuth 2.0 with an existing IAM solution is understanding the capabilities and limitations of the current environment. For instance, if the organization's IAM system is primarily designed for single sign-on to web-based applications using SAML or a custom authentication protocol, it may lack native support for issuing OAuth 2.0 access tokens. In this case, the integration effort involves introducing a new component—often an OAuth 2.0 authorization server—that can work alongside the existing IAM platform. This authorization server acts as a bridge, allowing the IAM system to remain the source of truth for user identities and authentication while handling OAuth 2.0 token issuance, validation, and revocation.

In scenarios where the existing IAM solution supports LDAP or Active Directory, the OAuth 2.0 authorization server can be configured to authenticate users against these directories. When a user attempts to access a protected resource, the authorization server forwards the authentication request to the IAM directory. If the user successfully authenticates, the authorization server issues an access token that grants the appropriate level of access. This approach ensures that user credentials remain managed by the established IAM system, maintaining consistency in account provisioning, password policies, and user lifecycle management. It also simplifies the integration process since the organization doesn't need to duplicate user data or change the existing identity provider.

For organizations using SAML-based SSO, integrating OAuth 2.0 often involves leveraging existing SAML assertions to issue OAuth tokens. When a user logs in through the SAML IdP, they receive a SAML assertion that proves their identity and includes attributes like user roles or group memberships. The OAuth authorization server can consume this SAML assertion and use it as a basis for generating an access token. This approach not only preserves the existing SAML authentication flow but also allows the organization to extend its SSO capabilities to APIs, mobile apps, and other services that rely on OAuth 2.0. By reusing the SAML infrastructure, the organization avoids duplicating authentication logic and maintains a unified user experience across all applications.

Another common integration scenario is when the existing IAM solution includes custom authentication workflows or proprietary APIs. In these cases, the OAuth 2.0 authorization server can be customized to call out to these proprietary systems as part of the token issuance process. For example, if the organization's IAM platform requires a custom challenge-response mechanism or an additional security factor, the authorization server can be extended to handle these requirements before issuing an access token. This flexibility ensures that organizations can adopt OAuth 2.0 without discarding the specialized security measures they've already implemented.

One of the key benefits of integrating OAuth 2.0 with existing IAM solutions is the ability to apply centralized policies and governance. Because the IAM platform remains the authoritative source of user identities, administrators can continue to manage roles, permissions, and compliance policies in a single location. The OAuth authorization server can then enforce these policies by issuing tokens with the appropriate scopes or claims based on the user's existing attributes. For instance, if the IAM system assigns users to certain groups or roles, these roles can be mapped to OAuth scopes, ensuring that tokens reflect the user's current entitlements. This approach maintains consistency in access control and simplifies compliance reporting, as all policy decisions are derived from the centralized IAM platform.

Another consideration when integrating OAuth 2.0 is token lifecycle management. IAM solutions often have well-established workflows for account deactivation, password resets, and other identity lifecycle events. Integrating OAuth 2.0 ensures that tokens issued to users or applications are automatically invalidated when those identities are suspended or removed. By configuring the OAuth authorization server to query the IAM system or listen for events such as user deactivation, organizations can ensure that access tokens are no longer valid once a user loses their entitlements. This tight integration between IAM and OAuth 2.0 helps maintain security and reduces the risk of unauthorized access.

Organizations also benefit from using existing IAM audit and logging infrastructure when integrating OAuth 2.0. Most IAM platforms include detailed logging of authentication attempts, failed logins, and changes to user roles or policies. By extending this logging to include OAuth token issuance and validation events, administrators gain a unified view of all access activities. This comprehensive audit trail supports compliance requirements, facilitates incident response, and provides valuable insights into how resources are being used. Integrating OAuth 2.0 with existing IAM logging systems ensures that administrators can continue to rely on familiar tools and processes for monitoring and auditing.

Scalability and high availability are also critical considerations. Many established IAM solutions are already deployed in redundant, highly available configurations to support enterprise-grade authentication. By integrating OAuth 2.0 into this existing infrastructure, organizations can leverage the same high-availability and disaster recovery mechanisms. The OAuth authorization server can be deployed alongside the IAM components, ensuring that token issuance and validation remain operational even during system maintenance or outages. This approach reduces complexity and provides a consistent level of service for all authentication and authorization requests.

Overall, integrating OAuth 2.0 with existing IAM solutions allows organizations to extend the reach of their identity and access management investments to modern applications, APIs, and cloud services. By leveraging the strengths of both frameworks, organizations can achieve a seamless transition to standards-based authorization without disrupting their existing authentication workflows or compromising security. This integration provides a solid foundation for scalable, secure access management while preserving the flexibility and centralized control offered by established IAM platforms.

OAuth 2.0 and Social Login Integration

Social login integration allows users to sign in to applications and services using their existing accounts from popular social platforms, such as Google, Facebook, GitHub, or LinkedIn. By leveraging OAuth 2.0, applications can provide a seamless user experience without requiring users to create and remember yet another set of credentials.

Social login not only improves convenience for users, but also streamlines onboarding processes for developers, simplifies account management, and reduces the risks associated with password-based authentication.

OAuth 2.0 serves as the underlying protocol for most social login implementations. When a user chooses to sign in with a social provider, the application (known as the client) redirects them to the provider's authorization endpoint. The user then authenticates directly with the social platform, granting the application permission to access their profile information, email address, or other data. Once the user consents, the social platform returns an authorization code or an access token to the application, which can be used to retrieve user information. This exchange ensures that the user's credentials never leave the trusted domain of the social provider, enhancing security and protecting sensitive account information.

One of the main advantages of integrating OAuth 2.0 social login is that it eliminates the need for users to create separate accounts for each application. By enabling users to log in with accounts they already trust, such as their Google or Facebook credentials, applications reduce friction during the sign-up process. This simplicity often leads to higher conversion rates and greater user satisfaction. Users are more likely to engage with a service when they can quickly log in without creating and verifying a new username and password. In addition, since users already have strong credentials with their social providers, the burden of maintaining secure authentication—such as supporting multifactor authentication or password recovery—is offloaded to the provider.

From a developer's perspective, OAuth 2.0-based social login integration simplifies account management. When users sign in via social providers, the application can retrieve standardized user information, such as names, profile pictures, and email addresses. This data can be used to create or link accounts within the application's user database. Instead of managing multiple authentication flows and password policies, developers only need to handle the retrieval and storage of user profiles, as well as maintaining mappings between social identities and local application accounts. This approach reduces development effort and operational overhead, freeing teams to focus on building application features rather than managing complex authentication systems.

Security is a key consideration when implementing OAuth 2.0 social login. Since users authenticate directly with the social provider, the application never handles sensitive passwords, reducing the attack surface for credential theft. Additionally, social providers often offer robust security measures, including multifactor authentication, fraud detection, and regular security updates. By relying on these providers for user authentication, applications benefit from the providers' ongoing investments in security. However, developers must still ensure that the integration is implemented securely. For instance, using HTTPS for all communications, verifying the social provider's signatures on tokens, and following best practices for storing tokens all contribute to a secure implementation.

Another benefit of OAuth 2.0 social login is the ability to request incremental permissions and offer fine-grained user control. When a user first logs in, the application can request basic profile information. If the user later wants to share additional data, such as their contacts or calendar events, the application can present a new authorization request. This approach allows users to remain in control of their data and helps build trust between the application and its users. Developers can take advantage of OAuth 2.0's scope mechanism to clearly define what data is requested at each stage, ensuring transparency and enabling users to make informed decisions.

Despite its benefits, social login integration with OAuth 2.0 does come with challenges. One of the primary considerations is managing multiple social providers. Each provider—Google, Facebook, LinkedIn, and others—may have slight variations in their OAuth 2.0 implementations, including different endpoints, token formats, and supported claims. Developers must implement logic to handle these differences and ensure a smooth user experience regardless of the chosen provider. To simplify this process, many frameworks and libraries offer built-in support for multiple social providers, abstracting the complexities and allowing developers to focus on integrating a single interface for handling authentication.

Another challenge is dealing with changes or disruptions in social provider APIs. Social platforms occasionally update their OAuth endpoints, deprecate older versions, or modify the data fields they return. Developers need to stay informed about these changes and update their integrations accordingly. By keeping dependencies up to date and monitoring provider announcements, developers can maintain a stable and secure social login experience. Building the authentication flow to be modular and adaptable helps ensure that the application remains functional even as providers evolve their APIs.

To further enhance the user experience, developers can offer a choice of multiple social login options. By providing multiple providers, such as Google, Facebook, and GitHub, users have the flexibility to choose the account they are most comfortable with. This inclusivity often improves user satisfaction and broadens the application's appeal. However, offering multiple options also means handling additional complexity in the integration and ensuring consistent behavior across all providers.

In summary, OAuth 2.0 serves as the foundation for secure and convenient social login integration. By enabling users to sign in with existing social accounts, applications can streamline onboarding, reduce credential management burdens, and enhance security. While integrating multiple providers and keeping up with API changes requires effort, the benefits of higher user engagement, simplified account management, and improved trust make social login an attractive choice for modern applications. With proper implementation and ongoing maintenance, OAuth 2.0-based social login can significantly enhance both the user experience and the developer workflow.

Threat Models for OAuth 2.0 Implementations

Understanding the potential threats to an OAuth 2.0 implementation is a fundamental step in securing any authorization framework. By identifying and analyzing these threats, developers and security professionals can design systems that mitigate risks and maintain the integrity of their authentication and authorization processes. OAuth

2.0, while flexible and widely adopted, introduces various attack vectors that must be considered at every stage of the authorization flow. From token interception and replay attacks to credential leakage and unauthorized client access, a well-defined threat model helps ensure that every component of an OAuth 2.0 implementation remains secure.

One of the most prominent threats in OAuth 2.0 implementations is the interception of authorization codes and access tokens. These tokens, once issued, grant access to protected resources. If an attacker can capture a token, they can use it to impersonate the legitimate user and access sensitive data or perform unauthorized actions. Common scenarios for interception include insecure transmission channels, such as using non-HTTPS endpoints, and vulnerabilities in client-side storage mechanisms. To mitigate this risk, it is crucial to enforce TLS on all endpoints, ensure that tokens are never transmitted over insecure channels, and store tokens securely—using encrypted storage on mobile devices or secure cookies in web applications.

Replay attacks represent another significant threat. In a replay attack, an attacker intercepts a valid token and resends it to gain unauthorized access. Even if a token is short-lived, replaying it during its valid period can still cause damage. OAuth 2.0 mitigates replay attacks by encouraging the use of one-time authorization codes (in the authorization code flow) and by integrating additional verification steps, such as the Proof Key for Code Exchange (PKCE) mechanism. PKCE adds a code challenge and verifier to the authorization code flow, ensuring that only the original client that requested the code can exchange it for a token. By implementing PKCE, developers can reduce the likelihood of successful replay attacks, particularly in public clients and mobile applications.

Another common threat involves malicious or compromised clients. In OAuth 2.0, client applications are trusted intermediaries between users and resource servers. If a client application is compromised, an attacker could potentially steal tokens, misuse the scopes granted by users, or exploit the client's credentials. To mitigate this risk, organizations should implement strict client registration processes, enforce least-privilege principles by granting only the minimum necessary scopes, and regularly audit and rotate client credentials. By reducing the trust placed in individual clients and implementing robust monitoring and alerting, developers can prevent or detect unauthorized actions by compromised applications.

Credential leakage is another critical threat to consider. While OAuth 2.0 is designed to avoid direct credential sharing, scenarios still exist where credentials can be inadvertently exposed. For example, client IDs and secrets may be hardcoded into applications or stored in publicly accessible repositories. If these credentials are leaked, attackers can impersonate the client and obtain tokens. To address this risk, developers should treat client secrets as sensitive data, store them securely (such as in environment variables or dedicated secret management systems), and never expose them in client-side code. Furthermore, using dynamic client registration and regularly rotating secrets ensures that even if a credential is leaked, its impact is minimized.

Token revocation and rotation also play a key role in mitigating threats. An attacker who obtains an access token can continue to use it until it expires. To reduce the risk, organizations should implement short token lifetimes and rely on refresh tokens to maintain sessions. In the event of suspicious activity, immediate token revocation and rotation can prevent further abuse. Monitoring token usage patterns, identifying anomalies such as tokens used from unexpected locations, and quickly revoking those tokens can significantly reduce the window of opportunity for attackers.

Phishing attacks targeting OAuth 2.0 implementations are another important consideration. Attackers may create fake authorization endpoints or consent screens to trick users into granting access to malicious applications. These attacks rely on social engineering to steal tokens or credentials. Educating users, providing clear branding and trusted URL patterns on the authorization server's pages, and implementing anti-phishing measures such as domain validation help reduce the effectiveness of phishing attempts. Additionally, incorporating multi-factor authentication (MFA) adds another layer of protection against credential-based phishing attacks.

Cross-site scripting (XSS) and cross-site request forgery (CSRF) vulnerabilities can also compromise OAuth 2.0 flows. In an XSS attack, an attacker injects malicious scripts into a legitimate client application, potentially stealing tokens or altering the application's behavior. CSRF attacks, on the other hand, can trick users into performing unintended actions, such as authorizing an attacker's application. Mitigating these threats requires proper input sanitization, secure coding practices, and the use of CSRF tokens. Ensuring that OAuth 2.0 authorization requests include a state parameter tied to the user's session helps prevent CSRF attacks, as the authorization server will only process requests that match the expected state value.

Threats also exist at the level of the authorization server itself. If the authorization server's keys are compromised, attackers can forge tokens or manipulate token contents. To safeguard against this, organizations must implement strong key management practices, including the use of hardware security modules (HSMs), regular key rotation, and secure storage of private keys. Monitoring and logging all key operations, along with strict access controls, further enhance the security of the authorization server and its token issuance process.

By addressing these and other threats through a comprehensive threat model, developers and security teams can build OAuth 2.0 implementations that are resilient against common attack vectors. Each component, from client applications to authorization servers, should be designed and maintained with security in mind. Ensuring secure token handling, implementing robust client verification, educating users, and leveraging proven security mechanisms like PKCE and TLS all contribute to a strong security posture. By proactively identifying potential threats and applying best practices, organizations can ensure that their OAuth 2.0 implementations remain secure, reliable, and trusted by users and resource owners alike.

Continuous Authentication and Session Management

Traditional authentication models often rely on a single event: the user logs in once, and that initial success grants them uninterrupted access until their session ends. However, as security threats have evolved, this "log in once, trust indefinitely" approach is no longer sufficient. Continuous authentication offers a more dynamic and adaptive strategy, assessing the user's identity and behavior throughout the session to maintain a high level of confidence. Combined with robust session management techniques, continuous authentication ensures that access remains secure over time without introducing unnecessary friction for legitimate users.

At its core, continuous authentication involves ongoing checks that verify a user's identity as they interact with a system. Rather than relying solely on static credentials provided at the start of a session, continuous authentication evaluates a combination of factors—such as behavioral patterns, device information, location, and risk signals—to ensure that the current user is indeed the same person who originally authenticated. If any of these signals deviate significantly from expected norms, the system can prompt the user for reauthentication, request additional verification steps, or even terminate the session. This approach enables organizations to detect and respond to potential security breaches in real time, reducing the risk of unauthorized access.

One common method for implementing continuous authentication is behavioral analysis. By monitoring how a user types, moves a mouse, or navigates through an application, the system can establish a baseline of typical behavior. Over time, this baseline provides a reference point for detecting anomalies. For instance, if a user's typing cadence suddenly changes drastically or their mouse movements become erratic, it could indicate that someone else has taken over the session. Behavioral biometrics are especially effective because they operate transparently—users don't need to remember additional credentials or perform explicit authentication steps. Instead, the system continuously validates their identity in the background, providing both security and convenience.

Device intelligence and environmental signals also play a crucial role in continuous authentication. Modern systems often track the device being used, including details like the operating system, browser version, and IP address. If a session suddenly shifts to a new device or location without a known reason, this change can trigger additional verification steps. For example, if a user logs in from their usual laptop in one city and then, moments later, the session moves to an unfamiliar device in a different country, the system can prompt the user to verify their identity again. By continuously analyzing these signals, organizations can quickly identify and block suspicious activity.

Continuous authentication also benefits from integration with risk-based adaptive policies. Instead of treating all users and sessions the same, adaptive authentication adjusts security requirements based on the perceived level of risk. Low-risk sessions may continue uninterrupted, while higher-risk scenarios prompt for stronger authentication methods—such as a one-time passcode, biometric confirmation, or additional security questions. This approach allows organizations to balance user experience with security, providing seamless access when confidence is high and introducing additional steps only when necessary. By continuously evaluating risk, the system maintains strong security without frustrating users with constant prompts.

Effective session management is the foundation for any continuous authentication strategy. Sessions define the period during which a user can interact with a system without reauthenticating. Proper session management ensures that these periods are both secure and convenient. Key techniques include setting reasonable session timeouts, implementing sliding session expiration, and using secure cookies or tokens. For instance, sliding expiration extends a session's validity as long as the user remains active, reducing the need for frequent logins while ensuring that inactive sessions eventually expire. Combining continuous authentication with sliding expiration allows sessions to last longer without sacrificing security—users who maintain consistent behavior and remain on the same device can continue their session seamlessly, while suspicious activity triggers additional checks or termination.

Token-based authentication, often used in OAuth 2.0 implementations, aligns well with continuous authentication and modern session management practices. Access tokens can be issued with short lifetimes, encouraging frequent renewal and reducing the impact of stolen tokens. Refresh tokens enable seamless reauthentication in the background, ensuring that users experience uninterrupted access while the system silently revalidates their credentials. Continuous authentication signals can inform token issuance policies—tokens might be renewed without user intervention if the user's behavior remains consistent, but any deviation triggers a reauthentication flow. This dynamic approach ensures that sessions remain valid only as long as the user's identity is trustworthy.

Another important aspect of session management is session revocation. If a security event occurs—such as the detection of a stolen credential or a confirmed account takeover—the system must be able to immediately terminate the affected sessions. This requires a centralized way to track active sessions and quickly invalidate tokens or cookies associated with them. Continuous authentication signals often provide the initial indication of a compromise, enabling the system to take prompt action. By integrating session revocation capabilities, organizations can contain threats and prevent attackers from maintaining prolonged access.

User transparency and communication are also critical in continuous authentication and session management. While many checks occur in the background, it's important to inform users when security measures are triggered. For example, if a session is temporarily paused due to an anomaly, a clear message explaining why—along with instructions to verify their identity—helps maintain trust and reduces user frustration. Proactively communicating changes in session behavior, such as requiring reauthentication after a long period of inactivity or detecting a login from a new device, builds user confidence in the system's security measures.

In summary, continuous authentication and session management are integral to maintaining secure and user-friendly access control. By continuously verifying identity, monitoring behavioral patterns, analyzing device signals, and adjusting security requirements based on risk, organizations can ensure that sessions remain secure over time. Combined with robust session management techniques, including token rotation, sliding expiration, and session revocation, these strategies create a dynamic and adaptive security model that protects both users and systems from evolving threats.

OAuth 2.0 in Multi-Cloud Environments

In today's complex IT landscapes, multi-cloud environments have become increasingly common. Organizations deploy resources across multiple cloud providers to take advantage of specific features, improve reliability, and avoid vendor lock-in. While this approach offers many benefits, it also introduces challenges—particularly when it comes to securing access to APIs, applications, and data across these diverse platforms. OAuth 2.0, as a widely adopted authorization framework, provides the flexibility and standards necessary to manage secure access in multi-cloud environments, enabling organizations to maintain consistent authentication, authorization, and policy enforcement across multiple cloud providers.

One of the key benefits of OAuth 2.0 is its standardized token-based approach, which simplifies authorization across disparate systems. In a multi-cloud environment, each cloud provider typically operates its own identity and access management (IAM) services. By using OAuth 2.0, organizations can establish a consistent method for issuing, validating, and revoking tokens, regardless of the underlying IAM provider. For instance, an application running in one cloud can obtain an access token from its home cloud's authorization server and then use that token to access APIs or services hosted in another cloud. As long as the resource server in the second cloud can validate the token—often by checking its signature against a public key or querying an introspection endpoint—this seamless token exchange allows applications to interact across clouds without duplicating user credentials or custom authentication logic.

Token validation is a central consideration in multi-cloud environments. OAuth 2.0 enables multiple validation strategies, from self-contained JSON Web Tokens (JWTs) to opaque tokens that require introspection. JWTs are particularly advantageous in multi-cloud scenarios because they can be validated locally by any service that holds the correct public key, eliminating the need to call back to the issuing authorization server. This reduces latency and ensures that resource servers in different clouds can quickly confirm the authenticity and integrity of tokens. On the other hand, using opaque tokens with introspection endpoints can offer more centralized control, as it allows the issuing authorization server to revoke tokens or update permissions in real-time. The choice between these approaches depends on the organization's security requirements, performance considerations, and operational complexity.

Multi-cloud environments also highlight the importance of token scope and audience. In OAuth 2.0, scopes define the permissions associated with a token, while the audience specifies the intended recipient of that token. By carefully defining scopes and audiences, organizations can enforce strict access control policies across multiple clouds. For example, a token issued by a central authorization server might include scopes that allow reading data from a storage service in one cloud, while preventing write operations in another. Similarly, audience restrictions ensure that a token meant for one API cannot be used to access a different API in a separate cloud. This fine-grained control reduces the risk of unauthorized access, even in a distributed, multi-cloud environment.

Another consideration is managing identity federation between clouds. Each cloud provider may have its own identity provider or user directory, but multi-cloud deployments often require a unified identity model. OAuth 2.0, especially when combined with OpenID Connect (OIDC), can federate identities across clouds. For instance, an organization might have a central identity provider that issues ID tokens and access tokens. These tokens can be accepted by resource servers in multiple clouds, providing a consistent authentication experience for users and applications. By leveraging OIDC's standardized user claims and discovery mechanisms, organizations can ensure that all cloud services recognize and trust the same user identities, reducing complexity and administrative overhead.

Integrating OAuth 2.0 into multi-cloud environments also involves addressing security and compliance requirements. Different cloud providers may have varying security policies, data residency rules, and compliance standards. OAuth 2.0's flexibility allows organizations to implement consistent security controls across clouds, such as enforcing short-lived tokens, implementing token revocation mechanisms, and using secure transport protocols. This consistency helps meet compliance requirements while maintaining a strong security posture. For example, a company that operates in multiple geographic regions can issue region-specific tokens or apply regional policies to tokens used in different clouds, ensuring that data access complies with local regulations.

To streamline operations in multi-cloud setups, many organizations deploy a central authorization server that acts as a single source of truth for token issuance and policy enforcement. This central server integrates with each cloud's IAM services and issues tokens that are recognized across the entire environment. By centralizing token management, organizations simplify their authorization infrastructure and reduce the administrative burden of maintaining multiple, isolated token issuance processes. At the same time, this approach enables consistent policy application—such as requiring multifactor authentication (MFA) for certain scopes—across all cloud providers. The central server becomes the foundation for a unified, cohesive authorization strategy, making it easier to manage users, applications, and resources in a distributed environment.

Scalability and high availability are critical in multi-cloud environments, and OAuth 2.0 supports these requirements through its decentralized token validation capabilities. Using JWTs, for example, means that each resource server can independently validate tokens without relying on a central introspection endpoint. This reduces latency and improves reliability, as services can continue to function even if the authorization server experiences temporary issues. Furthermore, by deploying multiple instances of the authorization server across different clouds, organizations can ensure continuous availability and resilience. If one cloud provider experiences an outage, other instances in different regions or clouds can handle token requests and maintain seamless operations.

In addition to facilitating secure communication between clouds, OAuth 2.0 also supports use cases like service-to-service authentication, user delegation, and third-party access. For instance, an application running in one cloud might need to access a machine learning service hosted in another cloud on behalf of a user. OAuth 2.0's delegation model allows the application to request an access token with the appropriate scopes, ensuring that the machine learning service only receives the permissions it needs. This approach minimizes privilege escalation risks and maintains a clear chain of trust across multiple clouds.

OAuth 2.0's adaptability makes it an ideal choice for securing multi-cloud environments. By standardizing token-based authorization, enabling federated identities, supporting fine-grained access control, and simplifying token validation, OAuth 2.0 helps organizations maintain a consistent, secure, and scalable approach to authentication and authorization across diverse cloud platforms. With the right architectural strategies, businesses can ensure that their multi-cloud deployments remain agile, compliant, and well-protected against evolving security threats.

Case Studies and Real-World Implementations

OAuth 2.0's flexibility and widespread adoption have led to numerous real-world implementations that demonstrate its value across various industries. From consumer-facing social platforms to enterprise-level resource management, these case studies illustrate how organizations have successfully employed OAuth 2.0 to address their unique challenges, enhance security, and improve user experience. Examining these implementations reveals best practices, common pitfalls, and innovative approaches that can guide others in deploying OAuth 2.0 solutions.

One prominent example of OAuth 2.0 at scale is its use by major social media platforms to enable third-party integrations. Companies like Google, Facebook, and Twitter have built extensive ecosystems where users can link their accounts to external applications and services. OAuth 2.0 provides the foundation for this functionality by allowing third-party developers to request access to user data without requiring the user's primary credentials. Instead of sharing their passwords with every application, users grant limited permissions through OAuth scopes, enabling access to their photos, contacts, or calendars in a controlled manner. This approach not only improves security but also streamlines the user experience, as individuals can seamlessly connect their accounts and manage their data-sharing preferences from a central location.

The enterprise sector offers another set of compelling case studies. Many large organizations have adopted OAuth 2.0 to unify access control across diverse systems, including on-premises applications, cloud services, and partner APIs. For instance, a multinational corporation might rely on OAuth 2.0 to grant internal employees access to a suite of productivity tools hosted on multiple platforms. By implementing a centralized authorization server, the company can enforce consistent policies and manage access tokens for all applications. This setup reduces the complexity of credential management, simplifies user onboarding, and ensures that access rights can be revoked immediately if an employee leaves the organization or changes roles. Furthermore, using standardized OAuth flows, such as the authorization code grant, provides a secure and predictable way to integrate both modern and legacy systems under a unified authorization framework.

Another real-world example comes from the financial services industry, where regulatory requirements demand stringent access controls and auditability. Many banks and financial institutions have turned to OAuth 2.0 to meet these demands while supporting the growing trend of open banking. By using OAuth-based authorization frameworks, banks can allow customers to securely share their account data with third-party financial apps and services. In these scenarios, OAuth 2.0 scopes play a crucial role, ensuring that each third-party application only accesses the specific data the customer has approved, such as transaction history or investment portfolios. Additionally, the token revocation capabilities of OAuth 2.0 help financial institutions comply with regulatory standards by ensuring that access can be quickly terminated if a customer withdraws consent or if a security threat is detected. The clear delineation of permissions and robust audit trails that OAuth 2.0 enables make it a natural fit for highly regulated environments.

Healthcare is another industry that has successfully embraced OAuth 2.0. With the advent of electronic health records (EHRs) and patient-facing health applications, secure data sharing has become a critical requirement. Healthcare providers and technology vendors have implemented OAuth 2.0 to grant patients controlled access to their medical records and to facilitate data sharing among different healthcare systems. For example, a patient might use a personal health management app that requests access to their EHR from multiple hospitals. Through OAuth 2.0's authorization flows, the patient can grant access to specific portions of their data—such as lab results or imaging records—without exposing their full medical history. This selective access capability not only improves privacy but also ensures compliance with healthcare regulations like HIPAA. By leveraging OAuth 2.0, healthcare organizations can empower patients to manage their own health information while maintaining strict security controls.

In addition to these industry-specific examples, many smaller-scale businesses and startups have adopted OAuth 2.0 to streamline their authentication processes and reduce development complexity. For instance, a startup building a Software-as-a-Service (SaaS) product might use OAuth 2.0 to integrate with popular identity providers such as Microsoft Azure AD, Okta, or Auth0. This approach allows the startup to offload user authentication to a trusted third party, saving development time and enhancing security. By relying on OAuth 2.0 tokens, the startup can implement a scalable, token-based access model that grows with their customer base. Moreover, using OAuth 2.0's standard flows simplifies the integration of third-party applications, creating new opportunities for partnerships and extending the product's ecosystem.

Across all these examples, certain best practices emerge. One of the most important lessons is the value of well-defined scopes and permissions. Organizations that invest time upfront in designing granular scopes—aligned with their security and business requirements—find it easier to manage access, audit user activity, and enforce least-privilege principles. Another best practice is the consistent use of HTTPS and strong cryptographic methods to secure token exchanges and protect sensitive data. By following these practices, organizations not only enhance their security posture but also build trust with their users, partners, and regulators.

Finally, real-world implementations highlight the importance of monitoring and logging. Many successful OAuth 2.0 deployments include robust logging systems that track token issuance, token usage, and token revocation events. These logs provide critical insights into system health, user behavior, and potential security incidents. They also simplify compliance reporting and help organizations quickly identify and address issues. By incorporating logging and analytics into their OAuth 2.0 infrastructure, companies ensure that their authorization frameworks remain resilient, transparent, and accountable.

In summary, the case studies and real-world implementations of OAuth 2.0 demonstrate its versatility and effectiveness in solving a wide range of authorization challenges. By examining how different organizations and industries have adopted OAuth 2.0, developers and architects can gain valuable insights into best practices, avoid common pitfalls, and confidently apply this standard to their own use cases. With its ability to enhance security, simplify integration, and improve user experience, OAuth 2.0 continues to be a cornerstone of modern authentication and authorization strategies across industries.

Future Trends and Emerging Standards

As the digital landscape continues to evolve, the future of authorization frameworks, including OAuth 2.0, is being shaped by emerging trends and standards. These developments aim to address the changing security environment, improve user experience, and meet the demands of increasingly complex application ecosystems. Understanding these trends is critical for organizations looking to stay ahead of the curve and maintain robust, scalable, and user-friendly access control solutions.

One significant trend is the push towards more granular and flexible access controls. Traditional OAuth 2.0 implementations often rely on broad, static scopes to define what a token can do. However, as applications become more interconnected and microservices architectures proliferate, the need for fine-grained, dynamic permissions is growing. Emerging standards like OAuth 2.1 and the Continuous Access Evaluation Protocol (CAEP) aim to provide more responsive authorization models. CAEP, for example, enables resource servers to continuously evaluate access policies in real-time, considering changes in user context, device state, or environmental factors. This dynamic approach not only enhances security but also allows organizations to implement more sophisticated access control policies that can adapt as conditions evolve.

Another trend is the rise of delegated access models for non-human actors, such as service accounts, IoT devices, and machine-to-machine communication. While OAuth 2.0 was originally designed with user-driven flows in mind, the growing prevalence of automated systems calls for better mechanisms to grant and manage permissions. Emerging standards like OAuth Device Flow and the Token Exchange specification address these needs. The Device Flow simplifies authentication for devices without browsers, enabling seamless authorization for IoT devices and kiosks. Token Exchange, on the other hand, provides a standardized way to delegate and exchange tokens across different contexts, making it easier to implement service-to-service communication securely. As these models become more refined, they will play a critical role in supporting the next generation of connected devices and automated workflows.

The continued evolution of token formats and signing methods is another area of innovation. JSON Web Tokens (JWTs) have become a de facto standard for many OAuth 2.0 implementations, offering a compact and self-contained way to convey authorization data. However, as security threats evolve, so do the methods for protecting tokens. Emerging approaches, such as using proof-of-possession tokens or integrating more advanced cryptographic algorithms, aim to strengthen token security. Proof-of-possession tokens bind the token to a specific client or device, reducing the risk of token replay attacks. By tying the token to a cryptographic key held by the client, only the rightful holder of the key can use the token, even if it's intercepted. These advancements help ensure that tokens remain a secure and trustworthy mechanism for granting access.

Interoperability and cross-domain trust are also becoming increasingly important. As organizations adopt multi-cloud strategies and partner with external vendors, the ability to seamlessly integrate authorization across different domains is critical. Emerging standards like the Fast Federation Protocol (FFP) and extensions to OpenID Connect are designed to simplify identity federation and cross-domain authentication. These standards aim to reduce the complexity of establishing trust between identity providers and relying parties, allowing users to move fluidly between services while maintaining secure, transparent access controls. Enhanced interoperability ensures that organizations can scale their authorization infrastructure without being locked into a single vendor or platform.

Privacy and user consent are taking on a larger role as regulations like the General Data Protection Regulation (GDPR) and the California Consumer Privacy Act (CCPA) emphasize transparency and user control over personal data. OAuth 2.0 extensions and new standards are being developed to improve how user consent is handled, displayed, and managed. For instance, the User-Managed Access (UMA) specification, built on top of OAuth 2.0, empowers users to define their own sharing policies and manage who can access their data. By providing more transparent consent flows and fine-grained sharing controls, these emerging standards not only help organizations comply with privacy regulations but also build trust with users.

Another future direction involves the integration of zero trust security principles into authorization frameworks. As organizations shift away from perimeter-based security models, the need for continuous verification and context-aware policies becomes more pronounced. OAuth 2.0 is increasingly being combined with frameworks like the Zero Trust Architecture (ZTA) to enforce strict authentication and authorization checks at every layer. By integrating with continuous authentication and risk assessment protocols, OAuth 2.0 implementations can ensure that access is granted only under the right conditions, dynamically adjusting policies based on user behavior, device posture, or network context. This alignment with zero trust principles enhances the overall security posture, making it harder for attackers to exploit traditional trust boundaries.

As digital identities expand to encompass decentralized and blockchain-based approaches, OAuth 2.0 is also being adapted to support these emerging paradigms. Decentralized identity standards, such as those proposed by the Decentralized Identity Foundation (DIF) and the World Wide Web Consortium (W3C), introduce new ways to manage credentials and claims. By integrating with decentralized identifiers (DIDs) and verifiable credentials, OAuth 2.0 could become a key component in enabling users to prove their identity and share attributes across disparate systems without relying on centralized authorities. This approach has the potential to enhance privacy, reduce dependency on traditional identity providers, and empower users with greater control over their digital identities.

Finally, ongoing efforts to simplify and streamline OAuth 2.0 implementations are shaping the future of the standard. The development of OAuth 2.1 and its effort to consolidate best practices and eliminate deprecated features aims to make it easier for developers to implement secure authorization flows. By reducing complexity, standardizing key workflows, and integrating modern security enhancements, OAuth 2.1 seeks to ensure that both developers and end-users benefit from a more reliable, intuitive, and secure authorization framework. This continuous refinement ensures that OAuth remains relevant and effective as the demands of the digital world continue to evolve.

A Comprehensive Checklist for OAuth 2.0 Deployment

Deploying OAuth 2.0 is a multi-faceted process that requires careful planning, thorough configuration, and ongoing monitoring to ensure a secure and effective implementation. By following a comprehensive checklist, organizations can systematically address the key elements of an OAuth 2.0 deployment, avoid common pitfalls, and maintain a high standard of security and usability. This chapter outlines a detailed checklist that covers every stage of the deployment lifecycle, from initial preparation to post-launch maintenance.

Before deploying OAuth 2.0, it is important to establish clear objectives and requirements. The first step is to identify the specific resources that will be protected, the types of clients that will access these resources, and the user flows that will be supported. For example, determine whether the deployment will include confidential clients (such as server-side applications) or public clients (such as mobile apps and single-page applications). Also, consider which grant types are most appropriate—authorization code flow for user-facing web applications, client credentials flow for server-to-server communication, or device flow for IoT scenarios. Clarifying these requirements upfront helps ensure that the deployment is aligned with the organization's goals and minimizes the need for major adjustments later.

Once requirements are defined, the next step is to select the appropriate tools and platforms. Organizations should evaluate OAuth 2.0 authorization servers, libraries, and frameworks that best suit their environment. Key criteria include compatibility with existing infrastructure, ease of integration, and support for security features such as token revocation, Proof Key for Code Exchange (PKCE), and multifactor authentication. By choosing reliable and well-documented solutions, teams can reduce implementation complexity, enhance maintainability, and benefit from a robust support ecosystem.

Security considerations are at the heart of any OAuth 2.0 deployment. It is essential to enforce the use of HTTPS for all communication between clients, authorization servers, and resource servers. Insecure channels can lead to token interception, credential leaks, and other vulnerabilities. Similarly, organizations should implement strong cryptographic algorithms for token signing and encryption, ensuring that tokens cannot be forged or tampered with. Employing short-lived access tokens and rotating signing keys periodically further reduces the risk of token misuse. To address replay attacks, use mechanisms like PKCE with public clients and state parameters to prevent cross-site request forgery (CSRF).

Another critical aspect of the deployment process is proper configuration of token scopes and permissions. Scopes define what a token can do and which resources it can access. A well-structured scope design follows the principle of least privilege, ensuring that tokens grant only the minimum permissions needed for the intended purpose. For example, if an application only needs read access to a user's profile, it should not request full access to all user data. By defining granular scopes and strictly enforcing them, organizations can limit the impact of a compromised token and provide better visibility into who is accessing what.

Before going live, thorough testing is essential. Testing should include both functional and security validation. Functional tests ensure that clients can successfully obtain tokens, access protected resources, and handle errors gracefully. Security tests verify that the implementation resists common attacks such as token interception, token replay, and privilege escalation. Penetration testing, code reviews, and threat modeling exercises help identify vulnerabilities and provide opportunities to improve the overall security posture. Additionally, validating that the authorization server and resource servers correctly handle token expiration, revocation, and introspection ensures that the system behaves as intended under real-world conditions.

After the initial deployment, ongoing monitoring and maintenance are critical to maintaining a secure and reliable OAuth 2.0 implementation. Logging and auditing play a central role in this process. Organizations should ensure that all token issuance, validation, and revocation events are logged, providing a clear record of who accessed what resources and when. These logs are invaluable for detecting unusual patterns, investigating incidents, and meeting compliance requirements. Regularly reviewing logs and setting up alerts for anomalous behavior, such as a sudden spike in failed authorization requests or unusual access patterns, helps identify potential threats early and allows for swift mitigation.

Post-deployment, it is also important to keep all components updated and patched. Authorization servers, libraries, and frameworks should be regularly reviewed for security updates and new features. Keeping the software stack current reduces exposure to known vulnerabilities and ensures that the deployment benefits from the latest security enhancements and performance improvements. In addition, updating configuration settings—such as adjusting token lifetimes, refining scope definitions, or incorporating new security features—ensures that the deployment remains aligned with the organization's evolving requirements and threat landscape.

Finally, providing clear documentation and support for developers is an often-overlooked but crucial part of a successful OAuth 2.0 deployment. Comprehensive documentation helps internal teams and third-party developers understand how to integrate with the authorization server, request appropriate scopes, and handle token lifecycle events. Well-documented error messages and code examples make it easier for developers to troubleshoot issues and adopt best practices, reducing friction and increasing the reliability of applications built on top of the OAuth 2.0 implementation.

By following this comprehensive checklist—defining requirements, choosing appropriate tools, ensuring strong security measures, thoroughly testing, monitoring and maintaining the deployment, and providing robust documentation—organizations can achieve a successful OAuth 2.0 deployment that meets both current and future needs. Each step builds on the previous one, creating a solid foundation for secure, scalable, and user-friendly authorization processes.

www.ingramcontent.com/pod-product-compliance
Lightning Source LLC
LaVergne TN
LVHW051243050326
832903LV00028B/2557